SHAGGING
in the Carolinas

The Pavilion, Ocean Drive Beach, S. C.

The pavilion was originally built in 1936 by the Roberts family from Loris, South Carolina. One postcard places the pavilion in Loris, though the town is actually 30 miles away. For a time, a sign on the back declared its name as the Bowery. During World War II, an army guard outpost sat between the pavilion and the beach to watch for German U-boats. After the war, a warning to pilots was painted on the roof: "No Landing On Beach." Signs proclaiming "Skating," "Dancing," and "Bingo" touted the second-story skating rink, used to present bands for dances, and the three outside dance floors: on the left on this side of the Ferris wheel; on the right in the covered, open-sided hut; and in the center, near the top of the steps at the back.

ON THE COVER: Leon Williams mesmerized and appalled onlookers as he danced the dirty Shag in broad daylight on the back deck at Roberts Pavilion c. 1947. Leon worked summers at the Pavilion from 1946 to 1949, calling bingo at night and as a lifeguard in the day. Playing on the deck behind Leon is Jimmy Cavallo and his band. Cavallo's Fayetteville, North Carolina, quartet became the house band at Bop City at Carolina Beach in 1948 and 1949 and often presented "all night sessions" at Ocean Drive. In 1956, Jimmy and his Houserockers sang the title song in Alan Freed's movie *Rock, Rock, Rock*. (Photograph courtesy of Leon Williams and Forevermore Records.)

SHAGGING
in the Carolinas

'Fessa John Hook

ARCADIA
PUBLISHING

Published by Arcadia Publishing
Charleston SC, Chicago IL, Portsmouth NH, San Francisco CA

Printed in the United States of America

Library of Congress Catalog Card Number: 2004114132

For all general information contact Arcadia Publishing at:
Telephone 843-853-2070
Fax 843-853-0044
E-mail sales@arcadiapublishing.com
For customer service and orders:
Toll-Free 1-888-313-2665

Visit us on the Internet at www.arcadiapublishing.com

CONTENTS

ACKNOWLEDGMENTS

Acknowledgment doesn't fully describe how I feel about this project and the people who have been there to assist along the way. Once in a while, I'm profoundly grateful to have landed in this moment of history to be witness to a subject as fascinating as human social dance.

I'm grateful for that evening in the fall of 1975 when my future partner, Chris Beachley, and I sat in a bar talking and I saw a couple at the far end of the dance floor doing a dance that captivated me so much that Chris kept turning to see what had my attention. I was hooked, but didn't know how hooked I was for another five years.

A few weeks earlier, Boo Baron at Big WAYS took me to see my first Beach Music group, Billy Scott and the Georgia Prophets, at Paul's Lounge in Charlotte, North Carolina. It was an exhilarating evening. Exposure to a lot of music I didn't know combined with an unknown dance to music I did know produced a long-lasting desire to know more that I was unaware of at the time.

The first Shag DJ I knew (and secretly understudied) was Sandy Beach at Big WAYS on Sunday afternoons. My first Shag teacher was Wayne Hicks of Rock Hill, South Carolina, in 1980. He tried for two hours to teach me how to sugar foot at a Sand Flea Shag contest in Greenville, South Carolina. My following teachers were Susie Beaver in 1985 and Shad Alberty. Pioneer Lacy Moore told stories for hours on Saturday afternoons while we drank gin on the rocks with fresh tomato sandwiches. My expertise began taking shape with the help of Berkley Altman in Charlotte, and when Kim Maynard took me under his wing, I was unknowingly ushered into the tradition of a free-style Shag line that went back to the 1940s.

I am grateful to the thousands who listened to my programs over the years. They were all, in a very real sense, my teachers. They taught me more about the music and tradition than I could have gotten anywhere else. I'm grateful for the hundreds of interviewees who shared intimate details of their lives to enhance my understanding of the Shag culture.

We should all be grateful for newspapers, microfilm companies, libraries, and archivists. They make research an extremely fulfilling experience.

A very special thanks goes to my invaluable research assistants, Kay "Able" Maddox and Susan Trexler, without whom I could never have completed this book.

I'm enormously grateful to my friends and family who have indulged my passion and obsession for all these years, especially my mother and father, Ruby and Jack Knight, who were far greater inspirations in my life than I ever knew. And Kathy, my heart, my anchor, and wife.

INTRODUCTION

This has been a work of love, admiration, adoration, and passion. It is both a history of the Shag and a journey through the Carolinas in search of individual and social experiences called Shagging

Shag history reads like love letters written in the sand. It is public, social, and yet intensely personal. Like those briny love letters, the Shag expresses heady emotions that should be taken with a grain of salt. Some relationships seem to have "forever" written all over them. By the following season, though, the words have washed away; names have been forgotten. The Shag is a dance of friends and romances found and lost. Sometimes it's the beginning of a lifetime together.

Shag is also a game of romance, seduction, collaboration, and improvisation. It is a game of play. This may seem a frivolous distinction in today's world—which is exactly the point. Play was always seen as frivolous activity in the United States and other puritanical societies until about 120 years ago, when a few enlightened minds began to connect ideas of play with recreation and reintegration. In fact, they began to consider play as an essential component in the good life of anyone who would maintain their sanity.

Dancing has long been diagnosed as a symptom of the dreaded disease of frivolity. Note, however, that those who condemn dancing are often, if not always, unable to duplicate it in a socially acceptable form. Ofttimes they will excuse themselves simply by saying, "I've just never been able to do it." The fundamental equipment is shared by all of us: two feet, two legs, a torso, preferably a pair of arms, a decent blood flow, and painless joints. That covers most of the basic tools. So what do the denigrators of dance mean when they say they can't do it?

It has nothing to do with equipment and everything to do with attitude and mood. The secret of mood is that it is far more than just a feeling. It is also a predisposition that allows for some actions and forbids others. The mood of anxiety, for example, and the fear of negative social opinions and the resulting loss of status, is an infamous killer of dancing. Anxiety, when connected with dancing, is almost always a fear of doing it wrong. This anxiety often arises from the belief that human beings should do only what they are good at and nothing else.

In a carefree mood, dancing thrives, and so do invention and improvisation. When one is unafraid of social condemnation, one is free to make mistakes—thus to invent. Invention always includes mistakes and failures. To be carefree is to be open to learning and to have unrestrained self-expression.

Dancing, as a function of self-expression, reveals something of the soul. This is one reason Shagging is sometimes called soul dancing. We don't ordinarily attempt to reveal our souls. We try to control our conversations and interactions for specific social outcomes with little or no room for spontaneity.

Shagging also requires, at the very least, a minimum of mutual respect. If the dancers have known one another for awhile there may also be mutual admiration.

So what do we have so far as the rules of the Shag game? They are carefree-ness—the capacity to fearlessly coordinate action with another; inventiveness—a natural human trait when we allow our impulses; learning—in a fun mood, it is fast, easy, and powerful; freedom—fearless self-expression; intimacy—vulnerability arising from self-expression; and friendship—mutual admiration and respect produces friendship.

Shagging happens when two people hold one or both hands, move together out of a basic step accompanied by some ensemble improvisation and back to the basic in time with the music. The addition of complex steps, especially unplanned steps, can make the whole experience more playfully challenging if the intent is to stay connected with the tempo and beat of the song as well as one's partner.

In the early years, all this took place to some very racy music, which added an additional, delicious danger. For one thing, it was forbidden black music. For another, the music was sinful. It was about sex. By 1947 and 1948, sex was everywhere: "I Want A Bowlegged Woman" by Bullmoose Jackson, "Good Rockin' Tonight" by Wynonie Harris, "Fine Brown Frame" by Nellie Lutcher, "Big Legs" by Gene Phillips, and "King Size Papa" by Julia Lee were among the many songs that celebrated sexuality and drinking and set the boundaries of the playground that fostered Shagging and Shaggers. Not that all Shaggers were drinkers—most weren't—but they were unafraid to enter the darkness of taboos beyond the firelight at the edge of society.

Taken together, all these components generated a sense of mutual risk-taking—dancing on the edge.

One

SHAG
Dancing on the Edge

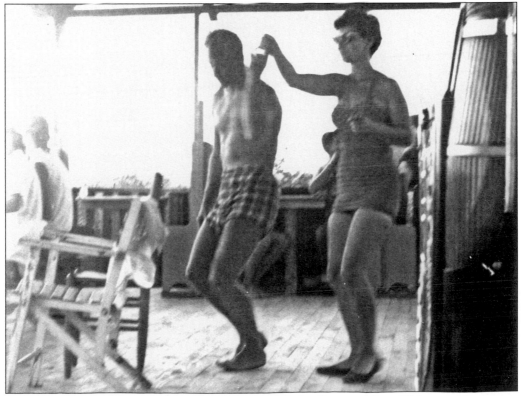

Marion Courtney of Laurens, South Carolina, and Ardis Courtney from Welcome, Minnesota, met in Detroit after World War II and moved back to Laurens. Avid Shaggers all their lives, Marion and Ardis enjoyed dancing at Buffington's Café on Lake Greenwood, South Carolina, in the late 1950s. (Photograph courtesy of Suzanne Kennedy.)

Lewis Philip Hall, pictured, wrote in his book, *Land of the Golden River*, "During the winter of 1927 your author, weary of the monotony of the foxtrot and the waltz, began to give some thought and time to a new dance geared to a different tempo and steps. With the assistance of a friend, who I will simply call Julia, since she is at the present a sedate married lady, we worked out a pattern of intricate steps danced to a double time beat. This dance routine we named 'The Shag,' and introduced it to the young dancing set during the second Feast of the Pirates festival in this city [Wilmington] in August 1928." Kay Keever, the wife of Jelly Leftwich, who played for the street dance where Shagging debuted, remembers singing with Jelly's band in Wilmington in 1930: "I jumped right off the stage and Shagged with Lewis—he invented the Shag, you know." Claude Howell, who lived in the same building as Lewis Hall, remembers that during his 12 years at Wrightsville Beach, "everyone down at the beach learned the Shag. We'd go to someone's porch at the beach and someone would show the rest of us. Then on to the Lumina and invent some more [steps]." (Photograph courtesy of Mary Jones.)

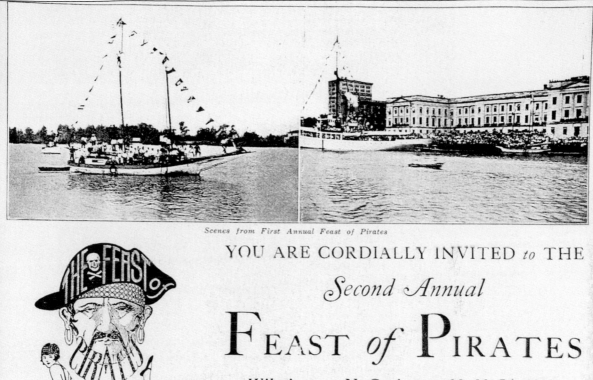

Scenes from First Annual Feast of Pirates

YOU ARE CORDIALLY INVITED *to* THE

Second Annual

FEAST *of* PIRATES

Wilmington, N. C., August 22, 23, 24, 1928

Fun - Frolic - Friendship

The Charleston was introduced to America indirectly from South Carolina in the early 1920s. Intrigued by the dancing of New York dockworkers in 1910, legendary stride pianist James P. Johnson used it 15 years later in "That Charleston Dance," a song written for Blake and Sissle's first Broadway musical. Lewis Philip Hall compares the dance to Shagging: "The Shag was entirely different in execution and rhythm, and it soon became so popular that the young people were dancing it everywhere, from tobacco warehouse dances to beautiful hotel ballrooms. . . . The Shag was not the smooth 'flat on the floor' steps of former years, but was instead a basic bouncing tap. It was really a combination of the 'Charleston,' Trucking and the Varsity Drag. . . . Following the basic, which was a shuffle, came a series of steps viz a swing. . . . Timed to the beat of the music, there was a fast Shag and a slow Shag. . . . The northern visitors, as well as southern vacationists, that came to Wrightsville Beach during the season went home after Labor Day and danced their version of the Shag, which was given other names."

Hours: 9 A. M. to 1 P. M.

JAMES-SHULL ANNOUNCEMENT

Friends throughout the state will be interested to learn of the announcement of the engagement of Miss LaBare Shull, of Shelby, N. C., to J. Stuart James, of Maple Hill, N. C. The wedding date has been set for September 10.

The engagement was announced at a party given at Shelby by Miss Elizabeth Riviere.

The bride-elect is the daughter of C. H. Shull and the late Mrs. Shull of Shelby. She received her education at N. C. C. W., where she made a brilliant record. Mr. James, who is a son of Mr. and Mrs. Gibson James of Maple Hill, is a graduate of Maryville college, Maryville, Tenn.

R. Y. P. U. to meet tonight.

The Senior B. Y. P. U. of Calvary Baptist church will meet this evening at 8 o'clock. Group 3, led by

"SHAG" DANCE CONTEST TO BE HELD TONIGHT AT WRIGHTSVILLE

Tonight's chief attraction at Lumina pavilion will be the annual shag dance contest which is being sponsored by Jelly Leftwich and his orchestra of Duke university. The contest is open to all dancers and already a large number of "shag dancers" have signified their intentions to enter this event.

A handsome prize will be awarded the winning couple in tonight's event. Impartial and non-resident judges have been selected.

WARSAW SCHOOL CLASS HONORED AT PARTY

WARSAW, Aug. 31.—Mrs R. E. L. Wheeless entertained at a lovely tea on the lawn of her home Monday evening, to honor the Warsaw

FASHION PENDULUM SWINGS BACK

The first reference to Shag in Carolina newspapers was on this society page from September 1, 1932. Although there were Shag contests every summer from 1929, they never made the local papers. (Courtesy of the *Wilmington Morning Star*.)

In *Land of the Golden River*, Lewis Philip Hall wrote: "By 1930, the Shag had been perfected by new steps. . . . The Shag reached its peak in 1932, and the managers of Lumina decided this dance also should have its place in the sun. The result of this decision was a Shag contest at Lumina, which traditional dancing contests in former years had been devoted to the two-step, fox-trot, and waltz." Here is one of the cups presented to the winners of the four dance divisions, which ended with the Wrightsville Shag contest in August 1932.

Although the Shag didn't show up in Carolina papers prior to September 1932, it did show up in numerous papers across the country. In this July 22, 1932, article, the writer for the *Ironwood Daily Globe* in Michigan embraces the Shag, the new dance in town. In an article from the *Chronicle Telegram* in Elyria, Ohio, an Associated Press writer predicted, " 'The Shag' . . . promises to exceed the Charleston in popularity. . . . Barred in New York, Philadelphia, Baltimore, Boston, and even nearby Richmond, 'the Shag' has retained its hold upon Virginia seashore resorts." (Courtesy of the *Ironwood Daily Globe*, Ironwood, Michigan.)

In Gotham

The Shag at Eve

New York—Quite enough has been said of the fickle aspects of fame. Still, I find it difficult to restrain this one additional instance. When the convention of dancing teachers opened at the Hotel New Yorker recently, announcement was made that the Lindy hop remained an outstanding ballroom dance. During the several days which elapsed, someone must have gone over the more recent dispatches. Toward the final session the statements read that the Earhart hop would be "the thing."

At any rate, cigars are no longer named after stage folk!

* * *

Speaking of the new dances reminds me that when the boy friend announces that he's going to a "shag party" you don't need to investigate his breath. He doesn't mean "stag."

This winter the shag at eve will have its fill. The teachers have decided upon the shag as one of the favored dances. I'm told that it's a mild form of tango and an improvement on the shuffle. Well the milder the better, so far as I am concerned. Yours truly in a tango is a fair imitation of a fly in tanglefoot.

Shag Contest Will Be Held This Evening

Lumina Event Will Be Final Contest For the Season; Program Planned

The "shag contest" tonight at Lumina will be the final contest of the season. A large number of couples have indicated that they expect to take part. This is the first contest of this kind to take place at Lumina and it is expected that a large number of spectators as well as dancers will be present.

"Guest night" last night honoring the visiting firemen who are here for their annual convention was enjoyed by many couples.

Thursday night Lumina will hold the final souvenir dance of the season and on Friday night one of the largest crowds of the season is expected to attend the Atlantic Coast Line Service club "Fall Frolic" and Fashion show.

Here, in an article written on August 28, 1935, in Wilmington, North Carolina, a Shag contest is reviewed. (Courtesy of the Bill Reaves Collection, New Hanover Public Library, and *Wilmington Morning Star.*)

"Shag" Night To Be Featured At Lumina This Evening

Special Music Has Been Prepared in Response to Numerous Requests

Tonight Hod Williams and his orchestra will give a specially prepared program of music for the "shaggers" at Lumina. Many requests have been made for a night featuring "shag" music. Dancing will start at eight-thirty and continue until one o'clock. Extra car service will be provided. Many out-of-town visitors and Wilmingtonians are expected to be present for tonight's week-end dance.

Last night's dance in honor of the fertilizer delegates was attended by a large crowd. During the evening a grand march was held and souvenirs were presented to all in the line of march. Many of the spectators as well as the dancers took part in the grand march.

Hod Williams and his orchestra were Shaggers' favorites in the 1930s as shown by this story in the *Wilmington Morning Star* on August 16, 1935. Hod also recorded one of the popular versions of the Big Apple in 1937. (Courtesy of the Bill Reaves Collection, New Hanover Public Library, and *Wilmington Morning Star*.)

Dusty steppin' is a dance that looks like Shag and is closely related. Ninety-nine percent of the participants are African Americans; many grew up in the dance's cradle city, Chicago. Many of the city's nightclubs play "Stepper's Sets" just for dusty steppin'—95 percent of these are Shag songs in the Southeast and other parts of America. (Story and advertisement courtesy of the Bill Reaves Collection, New Hanover Public Library, and *Wilmington Morning Star*.)

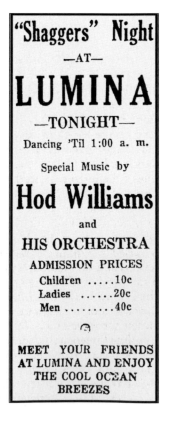

"Shaggers" Night
—AT—
LUMINA
—TONIGHT—

Dancing 'Til 1:00 a. m.

Special Music by

Hod Williams
and
HIS ORCHESTRA

ADMISSION PRICES
Children 10c
Ladies 20c
Men 40c

MEET YOUR FRIENDS AT LUMINA AND ENJOY THE COOL OCEAN BREEZES

The first mention of the Shag in a Charlotte newspaper was in this *Charlotte Observer* article from Sunday, December 29, 1935: "The young man on the left of my page is not Fred Astaire, but a pretty close second when it comes to tap dancing. He is Gerald Cummins of New York, one of the instructors in the Burkhimer School of the Dance. . . . Miss Bessie Burkhimer is recognized as one of the South's finest dancing teachers for children. To those youngsters who wish to learn the 'shag' steps, Onita Jean Mitchell, a Burkhimer graduate, will give lessons at a very reasonable price." Onita was a star pupil of Charlotte's Burkhimer School of the Dance. Bessie Burkhimer opened her first dance school in Charlotte in October 1905 and closed her second Charlotte school in 1937. Caroline Green, a student with the Burkhimer sisters in the 1920s, said they did not offer Shag in the early 1930s, except during the socials they provided on weekends for their students. (Courtesy of the *Charlotte Observer.*)

BURKHIMER
School of the Dance
214 1-2 Providence Rd.

Nationally Recognized

Announces

MID-WINTER TERM
Jan. 2, 1936

GERALD CUMMINS
Of New York

**EVERY TYPE OF THE
DANCE TAUGHT**

BESSIE V. BURKHIMER,
Directress
GERALD CUMMINS,
Associate Teacher
ONITA JEAN MITCHELL,
Assistant

na Shag, arranged for you by Helon Powell
oole of Charlotte, N. C. On your toes every-
ody—and let's *Shag* it!

Early this month, at one of her regular
lasses at the Twentieth Century Club in
ittsburgh, Mrs. Hubbell struck a novel note
introducing short snatches of the polka,
inuet, schottische and quadrille. She re-
orted that, after the session, pupils besieged
er with requests for an early repetition of
ese old dances.

The Ballroom Observer will ask Mrs. Hub-
ell to furnish explanatory notes and descrip-
ons for an early issue, and let's see whether
thers like these dances of long ago as well
s the Pittsburghers!

Next month we'll also have the *Beguine*
outine mentioned last month.

The Carolina Shag

Arranged by Helon Powell Poole,
Charlotte, N. C.

The *Shag* originated in the South. It is
anced mostly by the younger generation, the
igh school and college set. There are per-
aps a hundred variations, some of which are
ery intricate. Some of the steps are of
egro origin and there is no doubt that the
eps show this influence.

The fundamental steps are the *Kicking
tep,* the *Box,* and the *Triangle.*

The Kick Step

Step fwd. on L ft. (1). Kick R ft.
vd. (2). Step back on R ft. (3). Ball
nange L-R (&4).　　　　　　　　1 M

The Box Step

Step fwd. on L ft. (1). Cramp or
rop L heel (2). Step to R side on R
. (3). Close L to R (4).　　　　1 M
Step back on R ft. (1). Cramp R heel
2). Step to L side with L ft. (3).
lose R to L (4).　　　　　　　1 M
　　　　　　　　　　　　　　——
　　　　　　　　　　　　　　2 M

The Triangle

Step fwd. with L ft. diag. to R (1).
all-change R-L (&-2). Step to R on
. ft. (3). Close L to R (4).　　　1 M

Step diag. back to L with R ft. (1).
Ball-change L-R (&-2). Step to L with
L ft. (3). Close R to L (4).　　　1 M
　　　　　　　　　　　　　　——
　　　　　　　　　　　　　　2 M

The Strut—First Combination

One shag box step　　　　　　　2 M
Two kick steps starting with L ft.　2 M
Raise and lower heels (or jump in
place on both feet) (1-2). Tap L heel
diag. fwd. to L while raising and lowering R heel (3-4).　　　　　　　1 M
　　　(lady also uses L heel)
Return L ft. to R ft., raising and
lowering heels (1-2). Cross L over R
(both cross inside) (3-4).　　　　1 M
Cross R over L (1-2). Step to L on
L ft., sliding R ft. on floor (3-4).　1 M
Cross R over L (1-2). Step L (3).
Draw feet together and lower heels
(&4).　　　　　　　　　　　1 M
　　　　　　　　　　　　　　——
　　　　　　　　　　　　　　8 M

2nd Combination

Three triangle steps, starting with L
ft.　　　　　　　　　　　　6 M
Break: leap to R ft. and point L heel
fwd. (lady uses toe) (1-2). Leap to L
ft. and point R heel fwd. (3-4).　1 M
Three fast leaps R-L-R (1-2-3), hold
4).　　　　　　　　　　　　1 M
　　　　　　　　　　　　　　——
　　　　　　　　　　　　　　8 M

3rd Combination

One shag box step, starting with L ft.　2 M
Two kick steps　　　　　　　　2 M
Jig walk around to L away from partner L, R-L-R (2 cts. to step).　　2 M
Meet and lunge to L with L ft., knee
bent (1-2). Draw feet together, raising
and lowering heels to floor (3-4).　1 M
Repeat last M.　　　　　　　　1 M
　　　　　　　　　　　　　　——
　　　　　　　　　　　　　　8 M

4th Combination

Leap to L, brushing R ft. out to side
and landing on both feet (1). Cramp
heels (2). Cross L ft. over in front (3).
Step to R on R ft. (4).　　　　　1 M

Draw feet together (5-6). Cross
over in back with knee bent (7-8).
Lunge to L on L ft. (1-2). Draw fe
together and cramp heels (3-4).
Repeat last M.
Repeat last 4 M.

5th Combination

One shag box step
Two kick steps
Lunge to L (1). Slide feet togeth
(2). Raise and lower heels twice (3-4
Repeat last M.
Cross L ft. over R (1). R over L (2
L over R (3). R over L (4).
Lunge to L (1). Draw R ft. up to
(2). Raise and lower heels twice (3-4

6th Combination

Three triangle steps starting L ft.
Break: stamp on balls of ft. L-R-
(1 & 2). Shuffle R (& 3). Hop L (&
cross R over L in back (4), makin
half-turn R away from partner.
Turn and jig walk around to L an
face partner L-R-L-R (1-2-3-4).

7th Combination

Three kick steps with quarter-turn
L on 3rd kick (lady kicking fwd. wi
L ft. on last kick), conversational pos.
Change weight from R to L (1-2
Then to R (3-4) while making ha
turn to R.
Kick L fwd. (1-2). Step back on
(3). Ball-change to R-L (&-4).
Cross R ft. over L, making quarte
turn to L back into dance pos. (1-2
Cross L ft. over R (3-4).
Cross R ft. over L (1-2). Step to
with L ft. (3-4).
Draw R ft. up to L, sliding feet an
transferring weight to R ft. (1-2). Ba
change L-R (&3). Ball-change L-
(& 4).

In Charlotte's Fourth Ward, Helon Powell Poole was something of a quiet mystery. Even her cousin, Elsie, who had lived with Helon in the same house up through the 1920s, didn't know about Helon's impact on the 1930s and 1940s dance world. *American Dancer* magazine was the premier dance magazine in the first part of the 20th century. Helon was the first to explain the choreography of Swing in *American Dancer.* This story asserts Shag's origins in the South, but space for further explanation was at a premium. Helon almost certainly knew Lewis Philip Hall through her mentors, the Burkhimer sisters, who grew up in Wilmington and lived during the summers at Wrightsville Beach along with Lewis. The Burkhimers took their classes to the Lumina every summer after 1925 for special recitals. In the mid-1940s, Helon's son and daughter, Robert and Patricia, appeared in *American Dancer* as the youngest professional dance team in America. Patricia became one of the Radio City dancers, joined the early June Taylor dancers, and eventually raised a family with Dick van Patten. (Courtesy of *American Dancer* magazine.)

The Ballroom Observer

A Forum of the Social Dance Conducted by

THOMAS E. PARSON

THIS department was recently called upon to act in its reputed advisory capacity when a young ballroom teacher, serious enough about her chosen vocation to take advantage of every possible bit of information concerning ballroom dancing, inquired if it was technically correct to advise a pupil to step off on the left foot when the weight of the body was already on that same left foot.

Asked to clarify her question a bit, she produced a sheet of paper wherein were contained illustrated instructions for one of the newest motion picture dances and pointed out no less than two instances in the text matter directing the reader to commence a step with the left foot when the previous step had evidently been a transfer of weight on that same left foot.

Much has been said heretofore in these columns about the absolute necessity of a more comprehensible and uniform system of describing dance routines and steps in writing. It is to further this thought, rather than to criticize the system used in describing the dance in question, that the following analysis is offered:

In the first paragraph of text, there is described what is taken for granted as the key step of the dance, thus:

Huapango Step—Tap L heel in place (1), tap L toe in place (and) step on L ball of foot (2) hold (and)   1 meas.

HELON POWELL POOLE, *of Charlotte, N. C., is the latest teacher to broadcast lessons over the air. She is on WBT, Charlotte*

Helon Powell Poole taught the Shag and other dances over 50,000-watt radio powerhouse WBT. Helon was often a featured writer in *American Dancer* magazine in the mid-1930s, premiering the Big Apple, the Shag, and Swing dance in its pages. (Courtesy of *American Dancer* magazine, August 1936.)

JOHN SCOTT TROTTER
"Sheik"

Hi-Y, 2, 3, 4; President Hi-Y, 3; Boys' Cabinet, 3, 4; Home Room President, 3; Glee Club, 1, 4; President Glee Club, 4; Symphony Orchestra, 2, 4; President Symphony Orchestra, 4; Jazz Orchestra, 2, 3; Hi-6, 4; V-Pi Club, 1, 2; Secretary V-Pi Club, 2; Scribble and Scrawl Club, 3, 4; Treasurer Literary and Debating Society, 2; Marshal, 3; Vice-President S. P. Q. R. Club, 4; Vice-President Quenovalenada, 4; President Student Assembly and Student Council, 4; Class Lawyer, 4.

"If nature wishes to make a man estimable, she gives virtues; if she wishes to make him esteemed, she gives success."

To "Sheik" nature has lavishly given both virtues and success. So versatile is he that he presides with ease over meetings of the Student Assembly, stands high in scholarship, and when jazzing the piano, in presentday vernacular, he "paws a mean pedal." In school and in after life his sincerity of purpose and purity of character assure for him a true success.

HELON CLAY POWELL
"Pav"

Girls' Freshman Club, 1; Dramatic Club, 2; French Club, 3; Girls' High School Club, 2, 3, 4.

"Though our paths may lead a different way, We'll ne'er forget her for a day."

Helon's admirable personality and winsome ways have won numerous friends for her during her high school days. Her blonde curls and bright blue eyes make a most attractive combination. To know her is to admire her, for she is charming in manner. She is artistic and exceedingly talented in fancy dancing.

John Scott Trotter, music director for Bing Crosby for 30 years and a colleague of Swing stars Kay Kyser and Hal Kemp, was a graduating senior with Helon Clay Powell (later Poole) from Charlotte, North Carolina's Central High School in 1925.

MYRTLE BEACH HAS NEW DANCE

'The Big Apple', a Routine of Shag Steps Danced in a Circle, Newest Craze.

The newest dance craze, "The Big Apple", has hit Myrtle Beach with a whang. The dance was never heard of until a few weeks ago when somebody introduced it at the various dances on the beach.

The dance itself is a routine of shag and big apple steps. Several couples form a circle and go through a series of steps in time with the orchestra. Possibly the name, "The Big Apple", was given it because of the circle that the couples form. This same circle is maintained throughout the entire dance. It is said that a few weeks ago it was originated by a group of negroes in Columbia, S. C. This is signifi-ciant because one of the routines is called "Praise Hallelujah." This is where all the dancers in the circle more or less shag to the middle of the ring with their hands raised over their heads and in true ante-bellum style yell "Hallelujah."

In this 1937 *Charlotte News* article, columnist Dorothy Knox scooped everyone on the new dance coming out of South Carolina. The man responsible was Bill Spivey of Columbia, South Carolina, who had seen many of the Shag steps in a club called the Big Apple and who named his variation for that club. In this article, the writer points out that "the [new Big Apple] dance is a routine of Shag and Big Apple steps." The writer also stated, "the dancers in the circle more or less Shag to the middle of the ring." (Courtesy of the *Charlotte Observer*.)

Harry Fowler, one of the pioneer Big Applers, taught the Apple and the Shag. (Courtesy of the *Sumter Item*, September 22, 1937.)

Myrtle Beach News

Myrtle Beach, S. C., Thursday, July 22, 1937

IT'S "BIG APPLE" TIME AT MYRTLE BEACH

New Dance Originated Here or Hereabouts Sweeping the Country. It Wont Make Pies but its "Sweetest Ole Apple" Ever Bounced Around on the Floor. Young and 'Old do the Dance. Great Crowds Flock to the Pavillions.

The newspapers of the country, at least, many of them are having much to say about the "Big Apple" dance. Photographers have been rushed to this section to make pictures, and some of them have immediately become addicts, they caught the fever, and their temperature is above normal. It is a fever, it's a trance, it's the "Big Apple", and everybody with a spark of life likes the "Big Apple."

On Sunday night at the big pavilion, a few assembled, soon feet and bodies began to shake, hands to flip, and soon the new dance had the crowd.

It was during the rain that the fun commenced. The rain had suddenly commenced, and all those on the boardwalk took shelter. A dozen or more couples were riding on the Ferris Wheel, they had to "take it," and when they were finally dumped, wet and funny looking, they ran to shelter also, and why, nobody knows, for they were already wringing wet. But wait, listen to this, they joined the dancers, and when they finished, they were perfectly dry. Youth will have it's fling. Elsewhere in this issue there is published interesting articles telling about the dance. It is sweeping the nation.

Gov. Entertained By Horryites Here

Spivey Host to Enthusiastic Gathering at Plaza Hotel, Formerly Yacht Club Hotel

Due to the interest and enthusinsm for Myrtle Beach on the part of Collins A. Spivey and Mayor

AYNOR, (S. C.) RESIDENCE

—Photo by Perrin Kennedy

The above photograph shows the handsome residence of P. B. Huggins, Aynor, S. C. (Horry county). Mr. Huggins is a merchant and planter and is one of the outstanding citizens in Eastern South Carolina. Is also property owner at Myrtle Beach, S. C.

short addresses:

W. O. Gorwin, Harry G. Cushman, F. A. Thompson, Col. L. D. McGrath, E. S. C. Baker. These were followed by Governor Johnston, the guest of honor.

The local speakers were warm in their welcome to the Governor and often referred to Horry County empasizing the fact that "Horryites are noted for their loyalty, when they're fur you, they're fur you,

Asheville Member Of Local Real Estate Firm To Visit Myrtle Beach

Mr. and Mrs. Roy P. Booth and two young daughters, of Asheville, N. C., are expected at the Beach for a two weeks stay within a few days. Mr. Booth, who is a member of the firm of Booth & Little has notified Mr. Little of his proposed visit.

Horry County Board Of Public Welfare

Conway, S. C., July 20.—An examination for stenographic and clerical positions with the department of public welfare in the district which includes Horry County, will be held, beginning at 11:00 o'clock, a. m., in Florence, on July 23rd, in the commercial room of the high school on South Dargan street.

Candidates for stenographic positions are required to furnish their own typewriters, but other supplies will be furnished by the State department of public welfare. It will not be necessary that an application blank be submitted to take the examinations, as they will be competitive examinations open to anyone desiring to take them.

There will be two classes of examinations, viz: examinations for stenographic positions and examinations for clerical positions not requiring knowledge of stenography or typewriting.

Dean Of N. C. Medical Profession Visits Beach

Doctor J. P. Munro, Charlotte, dean of the medical profession in North Carolina, is a visitor at the Myrtle Beach residence, the "Charlotte Place," of Doctor James P. Mattheson. Dr. Munro's age is beyond the three-quarter century milestone but he is still more or less an active practioner. While here he will do some sight-seeing and visit "Inlet Acres," Dr. Mattheson's estate on Curlew Point, at Morralls inlet, S. C.

Lands Big Shark

Mrs. R. L. Brinson, High Point, N. C., Make Record Catch. Lands 400-lb Shark at South Island

Captain and Mrs. C. C. Beasley, Charlotte and Myrtle Beach, and invited guests, cruised south from Myrtle Beach on Tuesday to the jetties at the mouth of Winyah Bay, about fifty miles south of Myrtle Beach, and while fishing from the Annis III, a Richardson Cruiser, a yacht belonging to Captain Beasley, a member of her party, Mrs. R. L. Brinson, High Point, caught a 400-pound Sand Shark. Too much for one person to land, she was aided by others of the party in bringing the catch to the surface. Doctor Harrelson, Myrtle Beach, a will

While some regional newspapers ignored the new dance, it was front-page news in others. (Courtesy of the *Sun News*.)

Nightclubs discovered that Shag was a boon to business that had been slowly growing as the Depression subsided. (Glen Echo advertisement, August 4, 1937; courtesy of the *Marion Star*, Marion, South Carolina.)

The Big Apple's originator, 19-year-old Billy Spivey, leader of the Fanchon & Marco troupe and composer of "Big Apple Swing"

To all Big Applers, Billy Spivey

THE BIG APPLE

"PIGGY BACK"

"ORGAN GRINDER'S SWING"

→ "SCRATCHING FLEAS"

"SWING OUT"

AMERICA Big Apples! The latest dance sensation is sweeping the country! Theaters feature it, smart night clubs and hotels present it in floor shows! The younger set, and even the older, are Big Appling from coast to coast!

When Fanchon & Marco wanted a troupe of Big Applers, they went right down to its birthplace, Columbia, South Carolina, and signed winners of the Southern Collegiate Big Apple Contest, now playing in night clubs and vaudeville. Heading the group is Billy Spivey, credited as originator. And here Billy and his pals, Dottie Eden, Jean Foreman, Betty Henderson, Creighton Spivey and Kenneth Clarke, show you how to do it!

"Big Apple" is really nothing more than the old square dance with new steps thrown in—such new ones

as Truckin', Susie Charleston.

There is a "leade the figures. The circle, begin "swin the calls, with such as "Spank yo' Ho Fleas," "Organ G and "Piggy Back." man calls a name, to the center of "shines," which is name for a solo. leaderman says "P dance is over—unti

Billy explains ho dance. He went to night club and sa negroes dance. them, he got the duced it at his high spread to the Univ Carolina, then thre and now across the

18

"TRUCKING"

"SHINE, BILLY"

"SWING HIGH"

"SUSIE Q"

eckin' and

who calls
start in a
and follow
ting names
"Scratchin'
s Swing,"
the leader-
erson goes
circle and
Big Apple
when the
Allah," the
next set!
created the
Big Apple'
group of
watching
He intro-
l prom. It
of South
the South,
e country.

19

Big Applers gathered at the Myrtle Beach, Pawley's Island, and Folly Beach Pavilions in the summer of 1937 while the dance captured the international imagination. Helon Powell Poole helped direct a selection process along with impresario and booking agent T. D. Kemp in Charlotte (he was bandleader Hal Kemp's brother). Some of the kids were chosen for a trip to New York, and others sailed to England. (Courtesy of *Song Hits* magazine, February 1938.)

The September 1937 issue of *Stage* magazine offered a picture of the Apple from the place where it originated, the Big Apple Club, a converted synagogue in Columbia, South Carolina.

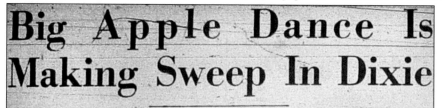

Big Apple Dance Is Making Sweep In Dixie

Charlotteans Taking Up Steps That Originated In Columbia, S. C.—It's Hard To Describe But You Know It When You See It.

By Floyd Wendell Cox

A dance now sweeping Dixie—"the Big Apple"—has finally settled in the toes and heels of Charlotte dancers at the Myers Park club and the Charlotte Country club has even tried it. Youngsters with a much lighter tap and springy rhythm may swing a little ahead of the old-timers but all manage to "truck" about and have carloads of fun.

Since many vacationers are returning to the city the "Big Apple" has become more in evidence for at the summer resorts this popular-over-night dance has been the rage amid the summer festivities. It is predicted that this dance will outlast in popularity the "Charleston," "Shag" and other seasonal dances.

Now the dance has spread over the south by students on vacation. Wherever a group of young South Carolinians gather you can hear: "Let's Apple." And, with old square dance style, a leader steps forward, the dances form a circle and the music strikes up.

"Right foot in," calls the leader. The dancers take a "Charleston" step toward the circle's center and back.

The *Charlotte News* predicted on August 1, 1937, that the Big Apple would outlast other "seasonal" dances of the past like the Charleston and the Shag. (Courtesy of the *Charlotte Observer*.)

In the August 7, 1937, issue of *Billboard* magazine, "The Shag" is number 18 on the chart. "Peckin' " and "Posin' " are tied at number 20—both are Shag steps adopted and adapted by Big Applers. (Courtesy of *Billboard* magazine, New York.)

Shep Fields recorded "The Shag" on July 2, 1937, for Bluebird records. His was one of two vocals that were released that year.

Songs With Most Radio Plugs

(A WEEKLY FEATURE)

Songs listed below are those which received six or more plugs on the networks, WJZ and WEAF (NBC) and WABC (CBS), between 8 a.m. and 1 a.m. daily, from Friday, July 23, thru Thursday, July 29, and also, for comparative purposes, from Friday, July 16, thru Thursday, July 22. Ratings are based on the number of combined network plugs for each song.

Also listed under Independent Plugs are the combined plugs for each song on WOR, WNEW, WMCA and WHN for the same period.

The symbol "F" after the title of a song denotes it originated in a film; symbol "M" indicates derivation from a musical production.

This census is collated and compiled by The Billboard staff from data supplied to The Billboard by the Accurate Reporting Service.

Position	Title	Publisher	July 23-29 Net.	July 23-29 Ind.	July 16-22 Net.	July 16-22 Ind.
1.	It Looks Like Rain	Morris	32	12	40	19
1.	Where or When? (M)	Chappell	32	36	31	22
2.	Sailboat in the Moonlight	Crawford	29	34	20	23
2.	I Know Now (F)	Remick	29	18	20	19
3.	Merry-Go-Round Broke Down	Harms	24	26	27	21
3.	The You and Me That Used To Be	Berlin	24	20	15	20
4.	Whispers in the Dark (F)	Famous	22	11	20	13
5.	Stardust on the Moon	Marks	21	24	18	18
6.	Stop! You're Breaking My Heart (F)	Famous	20	11	18	12
7.	All God's Chillun Got Rhythm (F)	Robbins	19	19	14	15
8.	Satan Takes a Holiday	Lincoln	18	23	13	9
9.	Gone With the Wind (F)	Berlin	17	26	16	15
9.	Cause My Baby Says It's So (F)	Remick	17	21	14	7
9.	Yours and Mine (F)	Robbins	17	16	13	6
9.	Tomorrow Is Another Day (F)	Robbins	17	9	21	9
9.	Can I Forget You? (F)	Chappell	17	8	3	6
9.	First Time I Saw You (F)	Santly-Joy	17	5	29	6
10.	So Rare	Sherman Clay	16	17	22	19
11.	Our Penthouse on Third Avenue (F)	Feist	15	12	13	11
12.	Good Mornin' (F)	Famous	14	23	17	9
12.	Caravan	Exclusive	14	18	14	16
12.	Am I Dreaming?	Davis	14	7	11	3
12.	Harbor Lights	Marlo	14	5	10	6
12.	Miller's Daughter, Marianne	Shapiro, Bernstein	14	4	17	5
13.	Me, Myself and I	Words & Music	13	16	12	14
13.	A Message From the Man in the Moon (F)	Robbins	13	12	13	6
13.	They Can't Take That Away From Me (F)	Chappell	10	8	18	13
13.	Afraid To Dream (F)	Miller	13	4	1	4
14.	Till the Clock Strikes 3	Shapiro, Bernstein	12	12	11	7
14.	Smarty (F)	Popular	12	9	1	2
14.	Image of You (F)	Feist	12	3	12	5
15.	My Cabin of Dreams	Berlin	11	16	7	10
15.	I'm Feeling Like a Million (F)	Robbins	11	13	11	8
15.	Strangers in the Dark (M)	Crawford	11	11	13	11
15.	They All Laughed (F)	Chappell	11	10	10	6
15.	You're My Desire	Mills	11	7	15	17
15.	Lady From Fifth Avenue	Shapiro, Bernstein	11	6	9	9
15.	Dancing Under the Stars	Select	11	5	11	6
16.	Don't You Know or Don't You Care?	Feist	10	4	7	7
16.	Loveliness of You (F)	Robbins	10	3	6	2
17.	September in the Rain (F)	Remick	9	13	13	8
17.	Johnny One-Note (M)	Chappell	9	11	9	14
17.	Love Is Never Out of Season (F)	Feist	9	10	20	7
17.	Heaven Help This Heart of Mine	Chappell	9	9	8	9
17.	You Can't Run Away From Love	Remick	9	6	9	13
17.	You'll Never Go to Heaven	Donaldson	9	6	8	13
17.	Have You Got Any Castles, Baby? (F)	Harms	9	5	0	1
17.	Toodle-oo	Shapiro, Bernstein	9	3	16	6
17.	That Old Feeling (F)	Miller	9	3	1	3
18.	The Shag	Ager, Yellen	8	20	9	12
18.	There's a Lull in My Life (F)	Robbins	8	11	13	10
18.	When Two Love Each Other	Davis	8	10	8	11
18.	Love Me	Red Star	8	9	8	5
18.	Cuban Pete	Hollywood	8	7	9	8
18.	Moon Got in My Eyes (F)	Select	8	7	3	2
18.	Moon at Sea	Mills	8	4	7	4
19.	Night Over Shanghai (F)	Remick	7	13	10	9
19.	Having Wonderful Time	Paull-Pioneer	7	10	13	11
19.	Your Broadway and My Broadway (F)	Robbins	7	9	3	6
19.	Never in a Million Years (F)	Robbins	7	8	12	15
19.	Folks Who Live on the Hill (F)	Chappell	7	8	3	3
19.	Blue Hawaii (F)	Famous	7	7	10	4
19.	What a Beautiful Beginning (F)	Hollywood	7	6	6	1
19.	Love Is a Merry-Go-Round	Shapiro, Bernstein	7	4	4	1
19.	I Hum a Waltz	Miller	7	2	9	6
19.	I Can't Give You Anything But Love.	Mills	7	1	2	6
20.	Peckin' (F)	Mills	6	13	2	7
20.	Scattin' at the Kit-Kat	Exclusive	6	9	3	8
20.	Posin (M)	Chappell	6	8	5	4
20.	Born To Love (F)	Harms	6	7	6	4
20.	Honeysuckle Rose	Santly-Joy	6	6	7	3
20.	When Day Is Done	Warner	6	5	0	3
20.	Summertime (M)	Chappell	6	4	4	3
20.	Hot Lips	Feist	6	3	3	6
20.	How Could You?	Remick	6	0	2	0
20.	Last Night I Missed You in My Dreams	Gilbert				

Turn to our Amusement Machines Music Section, for listing of five best record sellers (Bluebird, Brunswick, Decca, Master, Variety, Victor and Vocalion) for the

The Winthrop *Tatler* yearbook of 1937–1938 shows the girls of Winthrop College, Rock Hill, SC—(one of the dancing-est schools in the Carolinas) Shagging on the left, Big Apple on the right! (Courtesy of the Winthrop *Tatler* 1937–1938, Delta Epsilon Kappa, Winthrop University Archives and Special Collections, Rock Hill.)

Benny Goodman claimed in his 1939 book, *Kingdom of Swing*, that he invented the music from which the Shag originated. Benny didn't realize it was invented in Wilmington, North Carolina, in 1927. However, he was clearly one of the kingly performers with Shaggers, Jitterbugs, and Lindy Hoppers in the mid- and late 1930s.

Two

PAVILIONS, POOLS, AND PADS

There have been four Myrtle Beach pavilions. The first was built around 1902 with a bathhouse a little south of the current pavilion and sometimes served as a fish camp. The second pavilion, built around 1907, was not on the beach but about a block and a half back, with a long connecting boardwalk to the Myrtle Beach Hotel, also known as the Seaside Inn. In 1923, an oceanfront dance pavilion was built on the site of the first, which had burned. Both of these were the nucleus of what became the Myrtle Beach Pavilion Amusement Park. Pictured above is the third pavilion, also known as the convention center. Around 1930, a shack was added on the side, sometimes referred to as the jukebox shack. It was enlarged in 1937 and burned on December 28, 1944. The new Myrtle Beach Pavilion—the poured-concrete structure with the famous Magic Attic and an even more famous jukebox—was built and opened in 1948.

Folly Beach, South Carolina, also had a pier and dance pavilion. The first pavilion at Folly Beach was built amid rumors of bootlegging on the island in the 1920s, but it persevered, and the top American bands played at Folly Beach for decades. (From the collection of Davie Beard.)

The Atlantic Beach Pavilion, boardwalk, pier, and Oceanfront Hotel at Folly Beach were built in the 1930s. The hotel and pavilion burned in 1957.

The first visitors to the Isle of Palms arrived by the trains of the Charleston Seashore Railroad Company on July 28, 1898. The renowned Isle of Palms pavilion burned in the 1920s and was replaced by a two-story structure with a dance floor. When it burned on September 13, 1953, it was never replaced. In its heyday, the Isle of Palms pavilion featured the finest entertainers. (From the collection of Davie Beard.)

Bob Crosby first played Charleston in 1933 and was popular in the Bladen resorts area of North Carolina. Legend has it that Bob told brother Bing he wanted into the business. Bing, along with John Scott Trotter and their good friends Kay Kyser from Rocky Mount and Hal Kemp from Charlotte, told Bob he needed to play the June German in Rocky Mount to launch his career, which he did. (Courtesy of the *Georgetown Times*.)

—*Two*—
Grand Dance Bands
Isle of Palms
"AMERICA'S FINEST BEACH"
PAVILION

☆ ☆

Tuesday, June 15th
9:00 P. M. to 1:00 A. M.
Bob Crosby
Personally directing his famous orchestra, always popular in the South.
Kay Weber, lovely featured vocalist, Eddie Miller and Ray Bauduc.

Saturday, June 19th
8:30 P. M. Until?
Lennie Hayton
A national favorite and outstanding among the big name dance bands.
Lennie Hayton and Paul Barry in person on a Southern tour.

MAKE A DATE FOR BOTH DANCES
Popular Admission Prices for Tuesday and Saturday
Only $1.00 plus tax
Under Same Efficient Management as Last Summer
ISLE OF PALMS HOTEL NOW OPEN FOR SEASON
Admission to each dance
ISLE OF PALMS, SOUTH CAROLINA

The first White Lake summer resort, opened by Robert Preston Melvin in 1901, hosted Johnny Long, the one-armed violin prodigy from Charlotte. Melvin Beach's new dance pavilion opened on June 27, 1935, and often featured Hal McIntyre's orchestra. Hal's daughter, April McIntyre, was the morning DJ at the first full-time Beach Music station, WRDX, in 1986. In 1967, White Lake's first Blueberry Festival showcased many Beach Music bands.

Swimming and Shagging simply go together. Among many pools that had jukeboxes for fast dancers and Shaggers were Sustar's Pool in Matthews, North Carolina (this advertisement from the 1940s); Lynrock swimming pool in Eden, North Carolina; the pool in Grace Park and Recreation Center in Statesville, North Carolina; Twin Lakes in Columbia; and Tony's Lake in China Grove (and Landis), North Carolina. (Courtesy of the *Charlotte Observer*.)

When Pope's Park opened on June 25, 1926, it was the first organized recreation facility in Dunn, North Carolina, with a swimming pool, dance hall, and picnic facilities. Bands played Saturday dances twice a month. Pope's Park closed during the Depression after the swim season of 1934. Williams Lake in Mingo was 13 miles from Dunn, 21 miles from Fayetteville, and 18 miles from Clinton. Clayton Williams built a dance hall there during World War II while working as a carpenter at Fort Bragg.

In the 1940s, super Shagger Harry Driver was often seen at Williams Lake as well as other local venues. Harry also managed the Men of Distinction, a band from Dunn. Robert Honeycutt leased the resort in 1965 for the teenagers who had been visiting an empty warehouse in Faison, North Carolina. On the Wednesday after Easter 1965, Bob Collins and the Fabulous Five played. Notable entertainers included Jackie Wilson, the Tams, Martha Reeves and the Vandellas, Billy Stewart, Mary Wells, and Barbara Lewis. (Photographs courtesy of Kristye McDonald and Robert Honeycutt.)

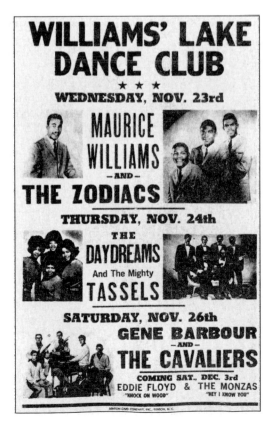

The Minnesott Pavilion was the home of the Minnesott Beach Bop, a local variation of Shag north of Morehead City in Arapahoe, North Carolina. Kids from Oriental and Pamlico County learned to dance to the two jukeboxes there. The original pavilion was built out over the Neuse River. Pictured from left to right are Ruby Croom, "Kid" Nash, and Nash's granddaughter, Ann Rouse. (Photograph courtesy of Ann Rouse.)

The Minnesott Pavilion was moved across the road after Hurricane Ione in 1955. According to Darrell "Dr. Dee" Sadler of Oriental, North Carolina, the pavilion was divided into a dance hall, patio/bar, and "Cozy Corner." The jukebox played pop and country music for dances held each Saturday most of the year. The Cozy Corner jukebox played "Rocket 88," "Big Ten Inch Record," "Lawdy Miss Clawdy," "The Fat Man," "60 Minute Man," and more. The pavilion remained open until the 1960s, when it was destroyed by fire. (Photograph courtesy of Garvin Hardison Jr.)

In Emily Weil's *The Dunes Club*, Marie Watson Cherry of Wilson, North Carolina, said, "We learned to Shag on that sandy floor by the jukebox which played all day every day." Marie said that in 1950, the waiters and bartenders, also teachers in Carteret County schools, taught her and her friends how to Shag. "The real cool boys were called Be Bops—it was the way they dressed, white buck shoes and ducktails, and we always danced the Shag." (Photograph courtesy of Emily Weil's *The Dunes Club 1940–2000* and the Dunes Club Collection.)

The Atlantic Beach "Circle" is pictured in Morehead City, North Carolina, in 1947. The Casino pavilion was built in 1931, burned in 1954, and rebuilt in 1955. At the top center is the Atlantic Beach Casino (later called the Pavilion). Earl Bostic was the first black entertainer to play there in July 1950. (Photograph courtesy of the Atlantic Beach Archives, Tom Doe.)

The Lafayette Court Pavilion opened in May 1935, several years after the demise of the first pavilion on Pawley's Island. On August 17, 1935, the Lafayette featured Cab Calloway's sister, Blanche, and her jazz band. In September 1932, another predominantly white Carolina venue featured a black entertainer: Don Redman played at Wrightsville Beach the same week the first Shag contest was reported in the *Wilmington Morning Star*. (Photograph courtesy of Bill Doar, author of *The Magic of Pawleys Island*.)

Opening Beach Dance At Pavilion Saturday

King Oliver and his Brunswick recording orchestra of fourteen artists will play for the opening dance at Pawley's Island Pavilion Saturday night, May 23, according to the management of the pavilion.

Although the beach season is not yet in full swing there are large crowds coming from nearby towns for the weekends and a large number of dancers are anticipated for the opening affair.

On May 23, 1936, King Oliver, a son of Savannah, Georgia, and the man responsible for inviting Louis Armstrong out of New Orleans to Chicago, played at the Lafayette. The *Georgetown Times* reported that Oliver played for "a colored dance" the night before at Georgetown's Palmetto Theatre. It may have been his last hurrah. Oliver had already lost his money to a Depression-era bank collapse and died in poverty in Savannah two years later. (Story courtesy of the *Georgetown Times*.)

After the Lafayette Pavilion burned in 1957, the people of Pawley's Island were concerned about their children riding the roads to Charleston or Myrtle Beach for entertainment. In 1959, they formed an association to build the latest—and last—Pawley's Pavilion, which opened on July 22, 1960. The new pavilion was built on the same spot as the old Lafayette Pavilion. Until it burned in 1970, the new pavilion featured many beach band favorites like the Rivieras of South Carolina.

The Pawley's Island Pavilion reunion has filled the night air with Beach Music and reunions of old friends and good times every May in the same spot as the Lafayette and Pawley's Pavilions from 1998 to 2005, thanks to Molly Mercer and friends.

The Lumina Pavilion in Wrightsville Beach, which opened on Saturday, June 3, 1905, was owned by the Consolidated Railways Light and Power Company. The railroad spur from Wilmington to Wrightsville opened in 1888. The 300-foot-long building included bowling alleys, a ladies' parlor on one side, and lunch booths, moving pictures, and slot machines. A wide staircase led to the second-floor dance hall measuring 50 by 70 feet and surrounded by another promenade 15 feet wide. At night, the building was illuminated by thousands of incandescent bulbs. Here, in the summer of 1928, Lewis Philip Hall and his dance partner taught the new Shag. They debuted in downtown Wilmington on August 22, followed by an all-night dance at the Lumina that night. Three dances in August entertained more than 30,000 dancers. From there, Shag spread northward and onto college campuses like wildfire. By the summer of 1929, the kids at Virginia Beach had declared themselves "Shag-mad," an early-20th-century way of calling oneself a fanatic or fan. (Photograph courtesy of Bill Creasy.)

Pocalla Springs supplies 29,000 gallons mineral water per hour. This beautiful resort is situated three miles south of Sumter, S. C.

Pocalla Springs in Sumter, South Carolina, often featured regional bands and Big Apple contests in the 1930s. Big Applers like Harry Fowler and Dot Bradford called Sumter home. Dot is an honorary member of the Shaggers Hall of Fame. Second Mill on the lake later became a hot spot for Sumter Shaggers. (From the collection of Davie Beard.)

Pullen Park, above, was in Raleigh, North Carolina. In and near Raleigh, many of the great places included Jim Thornton's Dance Club, Our Place, the Scrambled Dog, Stewart's Lake, Lake Merle, the "Y," and Teenage Frolics.

"During my early childhood, it was customary . . . to have an afternoon bath and don a fresh pinafore for a stroll with one's nurse to the drugstore for an ice cream treat and a trip to the park. . . . how many parents knew that their children's nurses, while out with their young charges, often dropped by Fred Green's . . . for a little socializing! . . . My first *live* exposure to black rhythm and blues," recounts Johnny Lou W. Fulmer in the Shaggers Hall of Fame Museum. (Photograph courtesy of the Andrews Museum and Town Council.)

The Twin Lakes dance pavilion, near Columbia, South Carolina, was another place to cool down in the summertime after the hot dancing in the pavilion's upstairs dance hall. (From the collection of Davie Beard.)

Buddy Nunn of Rock Hill was 15 the summer he heard this jukebox playing Wynonie Harris's "I Love My Baby's Puddin'" and other rhythm-and-blues songs. Bob from Pilot Mountain, North Carolina, drove hours to Spivey's after Hurricane Hazel in October 1954 to find that the only things left were a few boards and plumbing. There were three kinds of dancing popular at Spivey's Beach Pavilion—fas' dancin', slow dancin', and fist fightin'. (Photograph courtesy of Joan Owen.)

At High Point City Lake, the young and old in the North Carolina Triad area congregated on summers and weekends for Shagging and socializing.

The jukebox under the second-floor promenade changed thousands of young boys' and girls' musical tastes to rhythm and blues and Shagging when they heard and saw both for the very first time at the new 1948 Myrtle Beach Pavilion.

Myrtle Beach Pavilion's "board of trustees" is pictured c. 1948. These Myrtle Beach Chapin Farms employees at the opening of the new pavilion include lifeguards, concession workers, bathhouse operators, and sanitary engineers. The lifeguard third from the left in the front row is Al Munn, who owned the first full-time beach/oldies radio station, WIST, in Charlotte, North Carolina, from 1976 to the 1980s. (Photograph courtesy of the Society of Shaggers [S.O.S.].)

COASTAL CAROLINIAN

Myrtle Beach News

Week End EDITION

Myrtle Beach and Coastal Carolina
Has Highest Annual Sunshine Rating
in U. S by Government Records

A Frequent Return to Fundamentals Is Essential to the Preservation of our Liberties

VOL. 15 NO. 10   MYRTLE BEACH, S. C., SATURDAY, AUGUST 6, 1949   Subscription Price $2.50 Per Year

Police Push Cleanup Of 'Jitter Bug Bums'

Chief W. C. Newton of the Myrtle Beach Police Department said this week, in an interview with the News, that the clean up of so-called 'jitterbug beachbums' and vagrants, started last week with the chief's ultimatum to undesirables to get out and stay out of Myrtle Beach had been bringing satisfactory results.

Several persons with police records have been picked up

The necessity for stringent measures was further dramatized by the shocking kidnap murder of a Myrtle Beach taxi driver by two itinerants, and the brutal crowbar slaying of a transient laborer by a fellow carnival worker, during the past several weeks.

Chief Newton stated that the campaign was designed for the protection of vacationists, and was directed against those who had no visible means of

Fire Hazard Survey Shows More Hotels Safety Conscious

A comprehensive survey, last week, of hotels, guest houses, and motor courts to determine the proportion of fire protected buildings operated locally, disclosed that although adequately protected buildings were steadily increasing in number at Myrtle Beach there was still a group being operated which falls far below satisfactory safety standards. The survey was conducted by J. D. Edens, hotel and building inspector of

The unfortunate murder of two tourists by two itinerants led to a massive "cleanup" campaign in Folly Beach, Myrtle Beach, and Carolina Beach. New dance styles—especially the dirty Shag—the emerging class of beach bums, and the murders coalesced into a social threat characterized as "jitterbugs" in the minds of the authorities. Although the campaign didn't hurt Myrtle Beach tourism, dancers were driven out of Carolina Beach and never returned. (Courtesy of the *Myrtle Beach Sun News* and Horry County Memorial Library.)

PAGE'S LAKE NEAR FAYETTEVILLE; FORT BRAGG, LUMBER TON, ST. PAUL S, N. C.

BATH HOUSE, BALL ROOM AND DINING ROOM.

Page's Lake near Fayetteville was another proving ground for budding fast dancers. Inland lake pavilions and jukeboxes were often a more cost-effective way to "get away" for a weekend of Shagging without the costs of going all the way to the beaches.

Joan Simmons Opens Dance School
Here In Myrtle Beach Pavilion

Joan has been teaching for eight years in Charleston, and has recently opened a school in Georgetown. Miss Simmons has also started teaching in Myrtle Beach on Friday and Saturday mornings at 11 o'clock upstairs in the ballroom of the Myrtle Beach Pavilion.

Classes for new pupils of all ages are now being formed and will continue through the winter months.

Information may be obtained by writing P. O. Box 1237, Myrtle Beach, or by seeing Joan personally on Friday or Saturday of any week in the morning at the Pavilion at 10:45 a.m.

Tap, ballet, toe, acrobatic, musical comedy, novelty, baton twirling, singing, microphone technique, and ballroom including the shag will be taught. During the summer the pupils will appear on the kiddie program held on Monday nights in the Pavilion and many civic entertainments throughout the year.

Miss Simmons is professionally trained each year in New York by Jack Stanley, Fred Astaire, and Arthur Murray in whose studios she has gained recognition as an outstanding dancer and teacher.

Pictured here on July 21, 1950, Joan Simmons teaches Shag upstairs at the Myrtle Beach Pavilion. Joan helped her mother teach in Charleston in 1942 and opened her first school in Georgetown in 1950. In an interview in the mid-1990s, Joan said the Shag her mother taught in Charleston was the old hop, skip, and kick style from the 1930s (the Lewis Philip Hall Shag), but at the Myrtle Beach Pavilion, she was teaching the "get down and dig in the sand style from Spivey's Pavilion." (Courtesy of *the Myrtle Beach Sun News*.)

Sonny's Pavilion in Cherry Grove, South Carolina, was run by Sonny Nixon. Carolyn Mason graces the view above. Sonny's piccolo jukebox was legendary from 1949 to 1966. (Photograph courtesy of Sonny Nixon.)

Billy Ward and the Dominoes' bass singer, David McNeil from Wilson, North Carolina, remembered that the Dominoes played the Seabreeze Daley Breezy pavilion next to Carolina Beach two or three times in 1951 and 1952 after "60 Minute Man" hit the charts. (Photograph courtesy of Daniel Ray Norris, who grew up across the waterway from Seabreeze.)

Carolina Beach was a hotbed for dance in the 1920s, 1930s, and 1940s. Jim Hannah of north Mecklenburg County, North Carolina, arrived on a construction crew to help build the first pier at Carolina Beach, where he also met his sweetheart and future wife, Frances (at left). Jim's first dance joint was the Tijuana Inn, an innovative white establishment offering black music. Jim cut his teeth on blues on an old jukebox at the Frog Pond in Mooresville, North Carolina. Soon after the Tijuana Inn opened, a local dancer opened three "jump joints": jukeboxes chained down on the boardwalk with lots of black music. In 1949, Jim leased the second-floor ballroom of the Ocean Plaza Hotel as another dance hall (end of the street on the left, top photograph). (Photographs courtesy of Jim Hannah.)

The Tijuana Inn's jukebox sat right next to the front door on the right. Jim's tall and slim friend, "Chicken" Hicks, helped Jim name his new saloon after a road trip out west to California and Tijuana in 1944. Chicken traveled often to Seabreeze, the black beach a couple of miles to the north. He heard songs there that haunted him all the way back to Carolina Beach, where he had Jim call the amusement company in Wilmington to bring over those great songs for the "TJ" jukebox. Jim's second dance place, Bop City (named after "Hey Bop A Re Bop" by Wynonie Harris) became a legend from April 1947 into the 1950s. (Tijuana Inn photograph courtesy of Jim Hannah and Chicken's photograph courtesy of the Shaggers Hall of Fame.)

Roberts Pavilion was built by William Roberts of Loris, South Carolina, in 1936 and changed many times over the years. A bowling alley was added to the south side. Two dance floors were added to the beach side, one near the bath house on the left and one that included bands in the middle (shown on the front cover). Roberts Pavilion was totally destroyed by Hurricane Hazel in 1954. (Postcards courtesy of Sarah Richardson, North Myrtle Beach.)

At water's edge, Sarah Richardson of Albemarle, North Carolina, first visited Ocean Drive in 1949 with her parents. Her parents met at Spivey's Pavilion, where they danced. Sarah wrote in an unpublished work she is leaving for her grandchildren, "I was six years old when Hurricane Hazel took it away. . . . When Hazel came, on the morning of October 15, 1954, we were at the beach and I can remember the wind started howling. Sand had blown against the cottage door and made it near impossible to push it open. Without telephones or television, the pavilions were the place to go to find out what was happening. They were nailing boards on the front, music was playing on the jukebox and a couple was dancing, seemingly not wanting to 'give up' to a little storm that was coming. Dad decided it was severe enough and we left for Albemarle. It was good that we did, as Ocean front houses became intertwined with second and third row houses or they were just crushed beyond recognition. Robert's Pavilion was cut in half and Spivey's Pavilion was left with just a rusty water pipe sticking out of the ground." (Photograph and text courtesy of Sarah Richardson, North Myrtle Beach.)

Opening Day of the Pad ... July 4, 1955

Anxiously awaiting the delivery of the first beer truck. Front: Billy Moffatt (deceased), George Hall (deceased), Ben Umstead and Sonny Gillespie. Rear: Maurice Treadway and A.C. Brown Crook.

The Pad was the home of the North Myrtle Beach lifeguards' special society, called the KMA Club (one of this mystical anagram's meanings was "Knights of Many Adventures"). Maurice Treadway, the young man in the back row, was a Golden Gloves boxer and a generally mischievous young man around whom a thousand stories swirl. Kermit Turner's 1979 book, *Rebel Powers*, is based somewhat on some of Maurice's exploits. (Photograph courtesy of S.O.S. and the Association of Carolina Shag Clubs.)

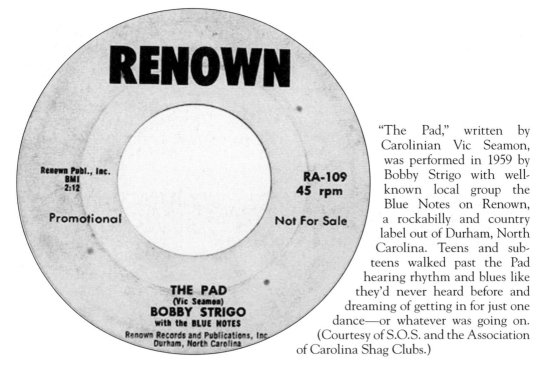

"The Pad," written by Carolinian Vic Seamon, was performed in 1959 by Bobby Strigo with well-known local group the Blue Notes on Renown, a rockabilly and country label out of Durham, North Carolina. Teens and sub-teens walked past the Pad hearing rhythm and blues like they'd never heard before and dreaming of getting in for just one dance—or whatever was going on. (Courtesy of S.O.S. and the Association of Carolina Shag Clubs.)

46

The Pad had several names and many owners. And the legends grew for nearly 40 years until it was razed in the early 1990s. One of the famous beach boys of the 1960s, Go Boy, said that even the pool table had a story (you needed to know at exactly what angle it was leaning if you really wanted to win). Above is an early photograph because it wasn't long before local citizens demanded that a latticework (below) be put up in front to prevent anyone from accidentally seeing the dirty Shag that was being danced inside. (Photographs courtesy of Lil John and Don Reid, the Living Legends Association, North Myrtle Beach.)

Smitty's Beach was on the Catawba River south of Charlotte. There was a jukebox for the early rhythm-and-blues edification of local fast dancers.

The Oasis Club was one of several establishments owned by Cooter Jennings that Shaggers of one flavor or another frequented in the Myrtle Beach area. (Photograph courtesy of Randy Jennings.)

Three

Readin', Writin', and Recess

The February 15, 1952, issue of the Winthrop *Johnsonian* shows "A smiling couple execut[ing] one of the latest Shag steps." (*The Johnsonian*, Winthrop University Archives and Special Collections, Rock Hill, South Carolina.)

Can You Imagine ?

...Walter Adams being a grouchy one-hundred-pounder?

...Joanne Elder being conceited and unfriendly?

...Bobby Simrill staring blankly into space after a good joke has been put over?

...Margaret Craig doing a fast "shag"?

..."E. M." Tucker saying that she will never read another book?

...The mess the Junior-Senior might have been in if it hadn't been for Gus Karres' hard work and original ideas?

...Anne Reese going with a Navy man?

...Bobby Dunbar sweetly agreeing with what everybody says, including Miss Williford?

...Baron Nowak being grouchy, unfriendly, and serious minded all the time?

...Velma Hearn, in horn-rimmed glasses, saying that she simply must go home to do her homework, for her A's are falling slightly?

...Anne McFadden telling a shady joke to the rest of the crowd?

...Ann White without "Brother"?

...The Goode Shoppe with a "No-U-Turn"?

...Carolyn Caveny cutting somebody off short?

...Barbara Bender faced in any direction except the Goode Shoppe?

...Clara Cooper not having a care in the world?

Can you imagine . . . "Tommy Merritt doing a fast Shag to 'Saphronia B'?" "Saphronia B" by Calvin Boze was one of the hottest Shag songs of 1950–1951. (From the 1951 *Garnet and Gold Annual*, Winthrop Training Institute, Winthrop University Archives and Special Collections, Rock Hill, South Carolina.)

The Shag showed up in 1950 in Rock Hill, South Carolina, in this annual: "Margaret Craig doing a fast Shag." (From the 1950 *Garnet and Gold Annual*, Winthrop Training Institute, Winthrop University Archives and Special Collections, Rock Hill, South Carolina.)

Can You Imagine

. . . Carolyn Moffat without a finger in every pie?

. . . Johnny Ward being a bookworm?

. . . Ann Pursley ignoring the males?

. . . Bobby Howe being a stern dignified senior?

. . . Cynthia Cauthen without her $17.50 uke or the hoof-to-mouth disease?

. . . Bobby Tarleton with kinky hair?

. . . Joyce McCall hurrying or being somewhere on time?

. . . Bill Grier not knowing where every penny of the class money is?

. . . Eva Williams being loud and noisy?

. . . Tommy Merritt doing a fast shag to "Saphronia B"?

. . . Ann Johnson with some scotch tape over her mouth?

. . . Jack Shaw calmly sitting on the side lines while a hot argument is in progress?

. . . Nancy Hutchinson being 6' 1" and weighing 200 lbs.?

The Winthrop Training Institute was a 12-year school run by Winthrop College as training ground for teachers at the college and for the children of college professors. The institute's students, Winthrop College students, and Rock Hill High School students obviously shared their preferences for music and dance. Here is the 1950 senior prom at Winthrop Training Institute.

The Winthrop Training Institute annual for 1950 and 1951 shows the students there already were calling their dance the Shag, and it can be seen in the photographs from their 1950 senior prom above. The 1953 class historian wrote in the *Bearcat*: "1950 . . . We had learned the dance called the 'Shag' that we'd wanted to do for so long, and now we were struggling with one of the oldies that had come back—the Charleston." (From the 1950 senior prom at Winthrop Training Institute.)

According to the 1952 Clemson *Taps* annual, "Shagging to the tunes of Beneke makes for an enjoyable evening" during one of the year's big dances.

In the 1952 Clemson *Taps* annual, "Ben Wright bites his lip as he attempts a tricky Shag step." Although publications of Clemson and Winthrop suggest that the Shag was going on well before 1952, the word itself is not in print in their prior annuals or papers. It is not surprising that the schools shared some of the same jargon; Clemson was a men's school and Winthrop a women's school. Because they were in close proximity in Upstate South Carolina, they came together for a lot of dances. (Photographs from the Clemson 1952 annual *Taps*, courtesy of Special Collections in the Strom Thurmond Institute, Clemson University.)

From the 1952 Clemson *Taps* annual, students dance "that Charleston Shag." In Charleston, Ashley High School's 1951 annual predicts that Beverly Donkerbrook would marry a Maharajah and that "he can 'Shag' too." The 1952 annual from Converse College in Spartanburg includes an apparently often-heard quote by senior Nancy Sue Carroll, "please teach me to Shag." The same annual has another quote by Nancy Ruth Phillips saying she "loves to Shag."

GEECH concentrates on a little of that Charleston shag. Tell that gal to let go of that dress.

SUGARFOOT, the big bad boogie boy, throws a real crazy shag.

The 1953 Clemson *Taps* annual shows "a real crazy Shag." The 1953 *Charlestonian* from Charleston High School includes a quote about senior Philip Chase that predicts his "cause of death" would be "Shagging, girls." (Photographs from the Clemson 1952 and 1953 annual *Taps*, courtesy of Special Collections in the Strom Thurmond Institute, Clemson University.)

Blue Monday Reveals WC Expressions That Are "The Most To Say The Least"

By JANET HORTON

The majority of us are unaware of the slang—both original and handed down—which makes up such a large part of our vocabulary here at Winthrop. A typical day can be humorously related with a touch of exaggeration.

The alarm goes off. Winnie sits up in bed, rubs her eyes, and immediately goes to the dub to wash her face. It is Monday; no wonder she feels just like the day after the week-end before!

She gets to breakfast just as the last strains of the blessing are heard. A hangover (don't misunderstand—at W. C. this results from a well-planned weekend) prevents her from exhibiting her customary talkative personality

ed to dust out her mailbox, but this morning, some object is intercepting the rays of light through the glass lid of the box.

Winnie's heart begins to flutter; then, she gets cold feet as she is trying to manipulate the box combination. Terrifying thoughts run through her head.

Was this a Dear John? A line from her favorite-guy-of-the-minute from Tigertown who had brought his old lady cowdet, a cold cat with pegged trousers and buck shoes?

Just as Winnie pulls the letter from the box, her mind is no longer in a state of suspicion. The address gives away the secret; it is a last-minute special offer from Time magazine.

right is satisfied with a tad. This, she exchanges, for a drag of their weeds. She says, "We ain't proud."

Bits of gossip are picked up in the atmosphere: "That thrills the very bones in my tongue . . . That was a low blow . . . you could' have gone all day without saying that . . . Someone told a funny . . . You act like a ninny . . . Want me to draw you a picture? . . . She's a foggy girl . . . Her tongue is loose on both ends . . . I have a trade for you . . .I . . . Drop dead . . . The crum! heard through the grapevine . . .

I think I'll live if complications don't set in . . . Pardon me for breathing . . . Oh, for a juke box so we could shag . . .

The Winthrop *Johnsonian* offered a guide to slang in its December 10, 1954, issue. In the second to last paragraph is: "oh for a juke box so we could Shag." (Courtesy of *The Johnsonian*, Winthrop University Archives and Special Collections, Rock Hill, South Carolina.)

A combination dance-party-card game is being scheduled by the social committee for the Saturday night following completion of examinations. There will be plenty of food, dancing, games, and juke-box music—so, guys, snag a hag, let's shag on out to Central Gym on Saturday night, March 21st.

The March 17, 1953, *Charlotte Collegian* contained the first appearance of Shag at the college. Jimmy Kilgo Jr., student body president in 1949 and graduate in 1950, earned a degree at the University of North Carolina and joined WIST in Charlotte. He started a specialty show called *Kilgo's Corner* and, in the 1960s, debuted his popular *Kilgo's Canteen* television show with Charlotte-area students vying for spots on the show. (Courtesy of the *Charlotte Collegian*, Rare Book Collection, University of North Carolina at Charlotte Library.)

CHARLOTTE COLLEGIAN

Vol. 7, No. 5   Charlotte College, Charlotte, N. C.   March, 1956

KILGO'S DANCELAND

The Charlotte College Social Committee went into much care and preparation to present to C.C. one of the most enjoyable and sociable dances ever to be presented at Charlotte College. The gymnasium was the scene of masses of swirling swinging dancers on the night of February 20 when Charlotte College was the site of a radio broadcast and at the same time a danceland haven.

The special guest at the dance was Jimmy Kilgo who presented his well known "Kilgo's Corner" program over station W.I.S.T. Instead of having an orchestra to "reel and deal" the music, the students were serenaded by varied musical arrangements played by the most popular instrumental and vocal groups of the country. Of course this music came to us via a hi-fi record player.

Jimmy is a graduate of Charlotte College. After having graduated from C.C. he attended the University of North Carolina to earn his A.B. degree in radio. While at U.N.C. Jimmy served as president of the Communication Club. Jimmy joined station W.I.S.T. in 1952 and has since built quite a name for himself around Charlotte and vicinity. As for his announcing qualities, tune to station W.I.S.T. and listen for yourself.

A coffee hour was presented in accordance with the dance and the guests had everything they needed for a special evening.

Another help in making the activity a success was the presence of nurses from Presbyterian Hospital who were invited to attend. The fellows that came stag didn't have any trouble finding a partner and we've heard that some good friendships blossomed from the occasion. In retaliation to C.C.'s invitation the Presbyterian nurses invited C.C. students to a dance at the hospital. There was a big response to this invitation also.

STUDENT COUNCIL

It was 8:05 o'clock on a Thursday night. The halls were quickly emptying and the noise and confusion was dying in the distance. I had time for just one more cigarette before crossing the threshold into a new world of unsolved problems.

Upon entering the library annex I became spellbound by the dead quietness of the people seated around the Student Council table. Right away the thought struck me that someone had died. But upon a hurried investigation into this impossible situation I soon discovered the cause for such a profound quietness. Darrel Avery was absent tonight. His Studebaker had became lodged between two ant holes and he was trying to get it out before the ants tore it to peaces part by part. He told me the other day that his car was the only automobile spoken of in the Bible. The Lord said "Have mercy on all creeping creatures."

The roll was soon called and Bill Vickery was asked to give a financial report for the quarter. This was a very precarious situation because Bill was in the middle of a deep snooze. After an eye opening moment he began searching through his pockets for his report. Bill Reid finally became annoyed and blasted out "I know good and well that we're not broke." Finally Mr. Vickery came out with the report. It was on the back side of an adding machine tape of which he had used to total his poker winnings of the night before.

Suddenly Ken Harris jumped out of his seat like Tarzan capturing gorillas and yelled, "The annual needs more money." Ann Padgett quickly retorted with, "Who do you think I am, Superman?"

John Scroggs was asked to give a report on the assembly committee and since he wasn't present at the meeting everyone took advantage of the opportune moment and a vote was taken to do away with the planned assembly. I'll give anyone in the Council two to one odds that he'll be at the next meeting with a shotgun.

The Student Council has been thinking of getting together outside of planned meetings for the purpose of getting things off their chests without taking up time at meetings. They have decided that if they can have so much fun together at the scheduled meetings that the fun they can have outside a meeting will be immeasurable.

After reading this column one might think that the Council is all fun and no work. If you think this you are only half correct. The Student Council controls all activities that are held at C.C. and also controls much of the money paid by the students for extracurricular events. If you have any "beefs" about what your money is being spent for, come and argue with us.

By the way, we'd like to say that Gus Travis doesn't have anything on this column.

FUTURE TEACHERS OF AMERICA MEET

The Future Teachers of America held their last meeting February 19, in the cooking lab. The purpose of the meeting was a discussion of the Special Education Department of the city schools. Many of the members of this group are in this field of teaching.

There were seven members present at the meeting and a number of members of the Delta Kappa Gamma, honorary society in education, who sponsored the meeting. The group also boasts of having one male at the meeting, Jim Babb.

Any one interested in the teaching profession is invited to attend these meetings.

FRESHMAN DANCE

Plans are being drafted for the Freshman Dance which will be held May 17th at the Elk's Club. Further information concerning this dance has not been released but should be known sometime in the near future.

PHILOSOPHY

Don't speak too harshly of your enemies. You made them.

ROOST GETS COAT OF PAINT

In order to keep the fashion trends up to the standard of equipment to be found in the Owl's Roost a new coat of paint has been added to the store. Now along with the ninety-nine, forty-four, one hundreths per cent pure cleanliness rating, the Roost can boast the same of the paint. Visit the Owl's Roost and see your friends.

This rare picture shows Jimmy Kilgo spinning the tunes. Kilgo furthered the popularity of rhythm-and-blues music through his "Record Roundup" column in the *Collegian* from September 23, 1954, to April 13, 1956. (Courtesy of the *Charlotte Collegian*, Rare Book Collection, University of North Carolina at Charlotte Library.)

The Shag was so popular it graduated from social status to part of the Winthrop curriculum for the students. (Courtesy of the 1955 Winthrop *Tatler*, Winthrop University Archives and Special Collections, Rock Hill.)

"We called it 'boogie,' 'Shag,' and 'kick it,' " recalls David Vaughan, president of the Ocean Drive KMA club. The picture is from his 1957 *Florentine* yearbook from McClenaghan High School in Florence, South Carolina.

Barbara Piner and Sam McGill, like other boppers (in much of Eastern North Carolina, "bop" was the word for "Shag"), lunched at Brady's to dance to the jukebox. They also bopped at the Scout Hut, Atlantic Beach Pavilion, Ducks, and Clarks at Atlantic Beach. Her favorite songs were the Dominoes' "60 Minute Man," Ruth Brown's "5-10-15 Hours," Stick McGhee's "Drinkin' Wine Spo-Dee-O-Dee," Fats Domino's "Ain't That A Shame," and Hank Ballard's "Work With Me Annie." (Courtesy of Dee Piner and Barbara Jeffrey.)

Georgetown Teen-Agers Enjoy Wednesday Dance
(Times Photo by Fleming)

Georgetown Recreation Facilities Have Busy Nights As Juniors Enjoy Dances

The Junior Canteen was started a few months ago for all children fourteen years of age and under. This program, supervised by Mrs. James C. Foster, is progressing well, according to Matt Goyak, Recreation Director of the City of Georgetown

"The attendance is getting bigger and bigger," the director said. "Some two hundred attended the Sloppy Joe Party held April 24."

The average attendance every Wednesday night is approximately 130, all being children under 14 years of age.

At the Sloppy Joe Party, prizes were given to the winners in the dancing contest. Carol Sprawls and John Thompson were the winners in a unique "shag" contest with Adrain Haigler and Kathrine Drew as winners in the slow dance. Judges for the contests were Mrs. R. A. Hemingway, Miss Pam Oyler and Miss Carolyn Day.

the older children go to the beaches. They have all the games as juniors, however, when attending the local recreation hall.

On Friday nights after the football games, the canteen is opened to the teenagers of the visiting team and at times 250 youngsters fill the Rek.

The facilities are available to the children from 2 until 6 in the afternoon in addition to these other hours.

Private birthday parties take up the extra hours when the Rek is not in operation. These parties are the only other activity that go on, other than the regular athletic program.

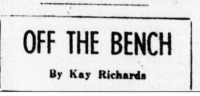

OFF THE BENCH

By Kay Richards

On May 9, 1957, after the Junior Canteen in Georgetown had been open for a few months, there was a special Shag contest. It was actually a contest honoring the best slow dance and the best Shag. Carol Sprawls and John Thompson won. (Courtesy of the *Georgetown Times*.)

BOCHETTE, ESSIE MAE, Orangeburg

B.S. Elementary Education

"Let's have some music" . . . third finger left hand . . . "my husband" . . . "Let's eat." . . . always ready to help . . . "Irby" . . . Shag fiend . . . one of the best.

Essie Mae Bochette, from Orangeburg, South Carolina, was a Shag fiend in 1958. (Courtesy of the Winthrop *Tatler*, Winthrop University Archives and Special Collections, Rock Hill.)

Clemson University hired some of the best orchestras. The Gladiolas, of Lancaster, South Carolina, played there for the first time in 1958. This picture was taken at the Clemson Spring Dance. The Gladiolas were Maurice Williams's group. Carolinians usually prefer the original version of "Little Darlin'," written by Maurice. Maurice wrote one of the most played and performed songs of all time, "Stay," in 1960. (Photograph from the Clemson 1958 annual *Taps*, courtesy of Special Collections in the Strom Thurmond Institute, Clemson University.)

A moments rest after that last shag.

The Shag was still part of everyday conversation at Winthrop as the 1961 *Tatler* illustrates in this photograph caption: "A moment's rest after that last Shag." (Courtesy of the Winthrop *Tatler*, Winthrop University Archives and Special Collections, Rock Hill.)

The beach was where many South Carolina students learned new Shag steps, and 1961 was a great year for Shag music. In December, the Raleigh, North Carolina, Embers recorded their first record, "I'm So Lonely." Charlotte's Catalinas recorded their first two records, "Hey Little Girl/Hey Senorita" and "Wooly Wooly Willie." Earl Bostic hit the charts a few months earlier with his smooth rendition of "Out of Nowhere." (Photograph from the Clemson 1961 annual *Taps*, courtesy of Special Collections in the Strom Thurmond Institute, Clemson University.)

"Now watch this step I learned at the beach last summer."

The crowded dance floor seemed to make the evening more enjoyable for everyone.

We could have danced all night but there are other things to do on dance weekends.

The mellow saxophone of Earl Bostic sent the dancers into a land of phantasy.

Provided with excellent music by Bostic, the couples settled down to a Saturday night of enjoyable dancing.

Earl Bostic's sextet furnished the music for the dance weekend. It was his first appearance on campus and his jazz left the students in awe.

Students are pictured Shagging at Clemson with Earl Bostic in 1961. (From the Clemson 1961 annual *Taps*, courtesy of Special Collections in the Strom Thurmond Institute, Clemson University.)

Clyde McPhatter and The Drifters drew what was believed to be the largest crowd at any Clemson dance.

Clyde McPhatter, The Drifters, Richard Maltby
Dates, Houseparties, Spirits . . . Homecoming Dance

Homecoming carries a magic sound which brings back fond memories to Clemson students. Not only did the Tigers beat the Tar Heels of North Carolina, but two talented groups performed for the dances that weekend. The dance floor was crowded Friday and Saturday nights with eager listeners and dancers who thrilled to the music of Richard Maltby, Clyde McPhatter, and the Drifters.

The highlight of the first night of the wonderful Homecoming weekend was the selection of the Homecoming Queen. Miss Diane Taft, the Beta Tau Sigma sponsor, was selected from a host of lovely beauties.

Friday night at the dance the students danced to the music of Clyde McPhatter and the Drifters. This night had been looked forward to for quite a while. Clyde McPhatter sang such favorite rock'n roll tunes as "Ta Ta" and "Money Honey." The dance ended all too soon at 1:00 Saturday morning.

After a fast Friday night and a field day Saturday afternoon to the tune of 24-0, the students and their dates were ready for the smooth, dreamy music of Richard Maltby and his orchestra. His music set the mood for a romantic climax to a perfect weekend. Midnight found the dancers starry-eyed and anxious for another dance weekend.

The Drifters hit, "Save the Last Dance For Me," was among the many great dancable songs heard by the large crowd.

Maltby's music is versatile. He has always been a favorite at Clemson.

32

The Drifters were a longtime Shag music favorite at Clemson. (From the Clemson 1961 annual *Taps*, courtesy of Special Collections in the Strom Thurmond Institute, Clemson University.)

Myers Park High School in Charlotte was a hotbed of Shag music enthusiasts. Several of the early members of the Catalinas and the Rivieras of North Carolina attended Myers Park. Ted Hall, a student and perhaps the secret understudy to booking agent T. D. Kemp (Ted's future father-in-law) first booked Maurice Williams and the Zodiacs for a Myers Park party in 1960. (Courtesy of the 1961 Myers Park High School annual, the *Mustang*.)

Rhythm on the River hit the big screen in 1940, starring Bing Crosby with John Scott Trotter, Crosby's music director and a 1925 graduate of Central High School in Charlotte, North Carolina. The lyrics show that Bing sang "how do you like 'Bugle Call Rag'? Played as a waltz or a Dixieland Shag?" Lewis Philip Hall said one of his best friends would call out, "Did you ever Shag to the Tiger Rag?" In 1945, Earl Bostic wrote and recorded "The Major and the Minor" for Majestic Records. The published lyrics include the words "Dixie Shag," but all recordings of the song are instrumental.

Two Raleigh, North Carolina, groups had the first Shag records of the modern era. Billy Bazemore and Keith Houston of the Band of Oz wrote the modern era's first beach song with Shag in the title with "Shaggin' " in 1979. The Embers' 1977 song "I Love Beach Music" was the first modern beach song to mention the Shag. Then the lid was off with a slew of songs, from Clifford Curry's "Shag With Me" in 1980 to Ernie LaBeau's "Everybody's Shaggin' " in 1985.

Jackie Gore (left) played parties around Hugh Morson Jr. High in Raleigh, North Carolina, with Robert Clayton on drums and Charles Burke on piano. Gore was co-architect of the Raleigh Embers with Bobby Tomlinson in 1958. Gore wanted to play his father's guitar for years, and he finally got the chance in this unnamed group, pictured in 1957. (Photograph courtesy of Robert Clayton.)

Gene Nobles started forming the legend of WLAC Nashville when he joined the radio station in 1943. He had a wry and sometimes subtly double-entendre sense of humor and DJ patter. By the mid-1950s, Nobles's show was a permanent fixture in the lives of many Carolinian teenagers. Monday through Saturday at 11:15 p.m. and Sunday at midnight, Nobles's theme song, "Swanee River Boogie" by Albert Ammons, opened his show, *Randy's Record Hi-Lights*, sponsored by Randy's Record Shop in Gallatin, Tennessee. (Photograph courtesy of Nikki Nobles.)

South Carolina's John R. (John Richbourg) joined WLAC as a newscaster in 1942, went to war in 1943, and returned in 1947. He signed on with: "This is John R., WLAC, Nashville, Tennessee, 50,000 watts strong, 24 hours long, way down south in Dixie." During *Ernie's Record Parade*, sponsored by Ernie's Record Mart at 179 Third Avenue North in Nashville, Richbourg sold baby chicks, Hoyt Sullivan hair products, and White Rose petroleum jelly. (Photograph and biography courtesy of Margaret Richbourg.)

WLAC's May 1953 program schedule marked former Little Rock, Arkansas, carnival bingo barker Gene Nobles's 10th anniversary with the Southern radio powerhouse. Fans took to heart Nobles's style and idiosyncrasies. Many could do one version or another of his Royal Crown Hair Dressing commercials. Everyone knew that his "cohort" was his engineer, and they couldn't get enough of Johnny Weissmuller's Tarzan yell that Gene lifted from Dale Hawkins's "See You Soon Baboon." (Photograph courtesy of Nikki Nobles.)

Bill "Hoss" Allen was a young drummer in the Air Force show *Flying Varieties* in 1943. After graduating from Vanderbilt in 1948, Allen did the *Harlem Hop* show at WHIN. In 1956, he took over the 10:15 p.m.-to-midnight spot when Nobles retired. The Hossman said that, in the early 1950s, he declined an offer from Randy Wood of Randy's Record Shop to invest in Dot Records. (Photograph and histories courtesy of Hoss's daughter, Bebe Evans.)

Radio stations nearly ignored both country and Shag music until 1940. When ASCAP licensing fees went up, radio stations formed Broadcast Music Incorporated (BMI) as an alternative licensing company in 1941. BMI began licensing country and black music, which ASCAP had largely avoided. Many called BMI "black music incorporated," as more "mixed" music aired on radio stations. Bands played rhythm and blues at square dances during intermissions in the 1940s and 1950s for "Shaggers" and other fast dancers. This newspaper advertisement ran on June 27, 1954. (Courtesy of the *Greenville News*, Greenville, South Carolina.)

Country music artists and the Shag were still romancing one another in 1958 when rockabilly artist Jimmy Crain released his writers' perspective on "Shaggin'."

Wally Mullinax played rhythm and blues on his *Ebony Swing Club* from 1950 until c. 1957. By 1954, though, his show became known as *The Chicken Shack*. His theme song and show opener were anthems in 1950. Wally used Joe Thomas's "Page Boy Shuffle" from September 1949 as he hit the air jivin': "From Charlotte, North Carolina—to Atlanta, G-A! And—Knoxville, Tennessee. To the sea! We're with it. And ain't gonna quit it!—Here—in the chicken shack! The shack's a-shaking, the joint's a-rocking, the fillies and chickens are dancin'. We're in the groove—REAL groovy. And Mel-oo-rooney. Get set for 30 minutes of gutbucket jazz on The Ebony Swing Club with . . . the ole Bee Bop King. We'll do the bee bop. And the Lindy Hop. Maybe do the shag. And—the ole rag mop. We'll boogie and woogie and have a ball, y'all!" Hugh Jarrett interned on *The Chicken Shack*, later becoming one of the Jordanaires behind Elvis, then Big Hugh Baby on WLAC Nashville. (From *Tall Tales, High Towers, Simple Ideas 'n Stuff*, by Wally Mullinax, 2003.)

WALLY MULLINAX
"EBONY SWING CLUB"
1:00 - 3:00 P.M.

MONUMENT
RECORDS

MO-513
Pub: Combine
Music Corp. - BMI
Time - 2:07

45-401

THE SHAG
(Is Totally Cool)
(Foster; Flood)
BILLY GRAVES

Another rockabilly artist, Billy Graves, recorded this 1959 release for Monument Records. In the 1970s, Billy Scott and the Georgia Prophets recorded "I Ain't Never," a remake of Webb Pierce's 1959 hit. Dallas Frazier's "Elvira" was a Shag hit in the 1960s and for the Oak Ridge Boys in 1981. "Cowboy Shag" songs crossed over throughout the 1990s. Country, swing, and Shag shared similar basic steps. Alabama put its stamp of approval on the crossover in their biographical "Dancin', Shaggin' On the Boulevard" in 1997.

Ray Charles, Ruth Brown, and other Atlantic Records stars had a "secret" link with the Carolinas beginning in 1950. Bert Fleishmann started a record distributorship in Charlotte in 1949, about the same time that Miriam and Herb Abramson of Atlantic were searching the South for a distributor. Black record stores flooded Fleishmann with reorders in the fall of 1949 for "Drinkin' Wine Spo-Dee-O-Dee" by Stick McGhee. The buyers were white kids who had heard the tune at the beach. Atlantic began using Carolina kids to gauge the "crossover" potential of new records.

Song Hits exclusively covered the white market beginning in the 1930s, but in October 1954, the publication announced that rhythm and blues was invading the pop field. Meanwhile, Hurricane Hazel destroyed Spivey's Pavilion, Roberts Pavilion, and other, lesser-known hot spots for dancers on South Carolina's Grand Strand. What started on the Carolina beaches nine years earlier—the musical mixing of two cultures—was becoming a national phenomenon.

Rhythm and Blues magazine emerged in October 1952. This is from December 1952, a year after Billy Ward and the Dominoes' "60 Minute Man" caused a furor in the radio world. This issue carries stories on Edna McGriff, the Treniers, Cardinals, Louis Jordan, Bull Moose Jackson, Buddy Johnson, Arthur Prysock, Nellie Lutcher, Joe Morris, Hal Singer, Lucky Millinder, Roy Brown, Dinah Washington, Freddie Mitchell, Little Esther, Willis Jackson, Mr. B (Billy Eckstine), Sonny Thompson, Camille Howard, Kay Starr, and Frankie Laine—a who's who of the Shag world.

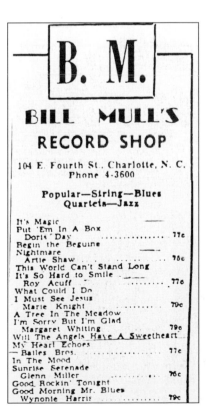

Rhythm and blues songs, or even lists of songs, were hard to find. *Billboard's* "Harlem Hit Parade" started in October 1942, became the "Race Records" chart in February 1945, and changed to "Rhythm and Blues Records" in June 1949. Occasionally record stores sprinkled rhythm and blues songs into their newspaper advertisements. Pictured is an August 1, 1948, advertisement listing Wynonie Harris, Toni Harper, Louis Jordan, Lonnie Johnson and Billy Eckstine. (Courtesy of the *Charlotte Observer*.)

Genial Gene Potts started playing rhythm and blues in 1948 on WGIV in Charlotte, North Carolina. It was one of a few radio signals in the area then. Known as the Olde Swingmaster, Potts was one of the most beloved of DJs in Charlotte. Many black schools made special dedications to him in their annuals. In 1955, the white students of Charlotte's Central High School voted him their favorite DJ and presented $100 to a children's clinic in Potts's name. (Photograph courtesy of Ed Myers.)

Pete Toomey started at WGIV as a gofer in 1953. Soon, however, there was need of a morning man from 5:00 a.m. to 6:00 a.m., and Pete took the job. When another opening came for 4:00 p.m., he was christened "Hound Dog" by the owner, and his star began to rise. The Hound Dog stayed with WGIV until 1965, when he joined the Charlotte Police Department. (Photograph courtesy of Pete Toomey.)

In 1948, "Chatty" Hattie Leeper became the first black female announcer in North Carolina at WGIV. She was an inductee into the BET Radio Hall of Fame in 1989 and the North Carolina Association of Broadcasters Hall of Fame in 2000. Hatty managed several Charlotte performers and opened Chatty's School of Communications in the 1990s. (Photograph courtesy of Hattie Leeper.)

Ed Myers joined WGIV from 1951 to 1954 to become a star newsman like Edward R. Murrow. Everyone at WGIV played a variety of music except Genial Gene, who played the rhythm and blues. Ed's *1600 Club* came on at 4:15 p.m., and his friends called and asked to hear the songs Gene played in the morning; thus Ed became the first white DJ to play rhythm and blues on WGIV. (Photograph and history courtesy of Ed Myers.)

WGIV — 1600 Kc.

5:30 Rural Rhythm	9:15 Nat "King" Cole	1:45 Quartet Calendar
6:15 Pete Toomey	9:30 Rhythm Express	2:00 Red Hot & Blue
6:30 Genial Gene	10:00 News, Hatty	2:30 Genial Gene
6:45 Coffee Pot Show	10:15 Chatty Hatty	3:00 News; Genial Gene
7:00 Genial Gene	10:30 Gospel Caravan	4:15 Club 1600
7:15 Coffee Pot Show	11:00 News	4:30 Ed Meyers
7:30 Genial Gene	11:15 Ruby Valentine	4:45 Club 1600
7:45 Minute Man	11:30 Blues 'n' Boogie	5:00 News; Car Tunes
8:00 News; Minuteman	12:00 J. Barber; News	5:15 Car Tunes
8:15 Julian Barber	12:15 Tops in Pops	6:00 Hour of Classics
8:30 Minute Man	1:00 News: Barber's Shop	7:00 Sign Off
8:45 Julian Barber	1:15 Barber's Shop	
9:00 News, Bing Crosby.	1:30 Glenn Miller	

The *Charlotte Observer*, like many newspapers of the time, published a daily listing of programs on local radio stations. Charlotte's four largest radio stations—WBT, WAYS, WSOC, and WIST—dominated the space. WMIT from Mount Mitchell and WGIV had fewer allotted column inches. This advertisement ran August 4, 1954. (Courtesy of the *Charlotte Observer*.)

RUSTY PAGE   Personal Manager
Ted Hall

Exclusive Booking Agent
HIT ATTRACTIONS, INC.
P.O. Box 682 Charlotte, N.C

Rusty Page was the 8:00 p.m.-to-midnight DJ on WGIV from 1957 to 1960 and drummed a bit with the Catalinas. He and "Hot Scott" Hubbs were the two white DJs of the period. After college, he returned to the morning show on WGIV in 1964 and emceed the legendary Park Center shows put on by Ted Hall of Hit Attractions. Page emceed the biggest names in rhythm and blues and soul of the 1960s and helped dozens of regional groups become Beach Music greats. (Photograph courtesy of Rusty Page.)

Triad area rhythm-and-blues DJ Gill announced, "Ah, this is Cirt 'Killer Diller' Gill, from around the city, it's 'Jam-A-Ditty' on the beautiful banks of the Buffalo." As a North Carolina A&T University graduate student, Cirt Gill was the first black DJ at a white station in the Triad area of Greensboro, Winston-Salem, and High Point. Cirt's *Jam-A-Ditty* show, named after a song written by Duke Ellington, played on 1400 AM WGBG from 1948 to his untimely death at 49 on December 18, 1960.

Oscar Alexander was "Daddy-Oh On The Patio" twice at WAAA in Winston-Salem beginning in 1957. He landed on the patio when WAAA and Ray's Roadside Drive-In joined efforts to generate more customer traffic. Daddy-Oh's show was punctuated with a jargon all his own such as "24 O'Roolies past 4 Mac Vouchers," and he was also known as "Yoh" and "The Good Ooch." His personality put the music he played over the top in the Triad area. (Courtesy of Mutter D. Evans, owner of WAAA.)

Oscar "Daddy-O" Alexander

When Billy Smith reigned king in the 1980s on WNMB-FM in North Myrtle Beach, he was also playing every weekend on the back deck of Fat Harold's on the ocean. The sign on the Tiki Hut above says, "On Deck Every Saturday Afternoon Broadcasting Live: Billy Smith's Beach Party." You hadn't really been to the beach if you didn't stop by Billy Smith's Beach Party. (Photograph courtesy of Becky Stowe at Beach Memories in North Myrtle Beach.)

The "Old B.S.-er," Billy Smith, has been a part of radio in South Carolina since the early 1960s. While working with WTAB in Tabor City, North Carolina (about a mile from the South Carolina border), the station ownership started a new station, WTGR, on the beach that became known as Tiger Radio, playing mostly Beach Music. Smith was named DJ of the Year at the First Beach Music Awards induction ceremony in 1982. (Courtesy of Born In the Carolinas Live Archives.)

Big WAYS in Charlotte contributed much to the growth of Beach Music. Jack Gale was program director and morning man. Long John Silver was later a big concert promoter, and Ron Brandon developed one of the big music tip sheets in the radio industry.

This brochure was for the Big WAYS Birthday Number 2 concert in 1967, which included Beach Music artists Robert Parker, Percy Sledge, Arthur Conley, and local heroes from Taylorsville, North Carolina, Harry Deal and the Galaxies, the first local group to become big at the Myrtle Beach Pavilion's Magic Attic. (Photographs courtesy of Ron Brandon.)

Musician Rufus Oates wanted to open a musical instrument center at the beach. He did with the Music Center in Myrtle Beach in 1963. Oates aimed to sell instruments and a few records. Folks kept asking for the Dominoes' "60 Minute Man," the Clovers' "One Mint Julep," and the Ravens' "Green Eyes." Rufus found and stocked them. By 1965, those songs and others had a new name—Beach Music—because folks understood them as coming from the *Beach Music* Center rather than Oates's intended Beach *Music Center.*

When Mr. Earl Husted started booking local bands into the Myrtle Beach Pavilion's Magic Attic, it became one of the most sought-after gigs in the Carolinas. The Duprees with the Pastels played there in the summer of 1962, with Willis Blume on drums (later to lead ShagTime and the Willis Blume Agency), Tommie James on piano (founder of Second Nature), Charles Stafford, Sam Camden, and Ronnie Turner. (Photograph courtesy of Julian Fowler.)

Buddy Skipper and the Jetty Jumpers showed up as one of the premier "carriers" of rhythm and blues in Wilmington, North Carolina, in 1958. The band was popular in Eastern North Carolina and made it to the Park Center shows in Charlotte a few times. They might have grown more popular, but as Buddy said, "We were like the farm team for the Embers out of Raleigh. Every time I turned around they were hiring another of my guys." (Photographs and history courtesy of Buddy Skipper and Wayne Williams.)

Skipper went national with the help of Marshall Seahorn from Concord, North Carolina. Seahorn went to New York, where he helped Bobby Robinson with Fire/Fury hire artists. Buddy joined other greats like Wilbert Harrison, Gladys Knight and the Pips, Sam Myers (today with Anson Funderburgh and the Rockets), Willie Hightower, and the Delfonics. Buddy had one of the biggest beach records of the 1980s with "Boogie the Joint" in 1986. (Record jacket courtesy of Buddy Skipper.)

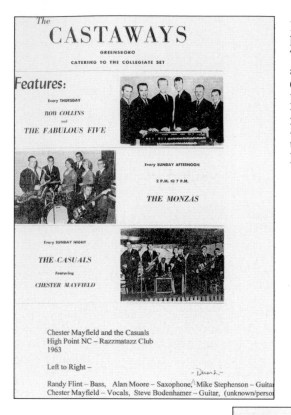

The Castaways
GREENSBORO
CATERING TO THE COLLEGIATE SET

Features:

Every THURSDAY

BOB COLLINS
and
THE FABULOUS FIVE

Every SUNDAY AFTERNOON

2 P.M. til 7 P.M.

THE MONZAS

Every SUNDAY NIGHT

THE CASUALS

featuring

CHESTER MAYFIELD

Chester Mayfield and the Casuals
High Point NC – Razzmatazz Club
1963

Left to Right –

Randy Flint – Bass, Alan Moore – Saxophone, Mike Stephenson – Guitar
Chester Mayfield – Vocals, Steve Bodenhamer – Guitar, (unknown/person

Bill Griffin was the "Man!" Everything he touched in the 1960s turned to gold. The Castaways lineup in 1964 was always as good as this lineup in September and October, which included the Tropics, Embers, Ascots, Weejuns, Dazzlers, Monzas, Casuals, the Fabulous Five, and Maurice and the Rebels. Bill later opened the equally awesome Bushes and the Hilton Underground.

The Castaways opened in 1963 as a teenage nightclub—no alcohol. The club was owned by Jokers Three Productions: a booking agency, record company, and the Jokers Three nightclub. The teenagers didn't come, so they tried to make it a college club. That didn't work, so they made it a black club. After Bill Griffin bought it in late 1963, the Fabulous Five played Sunday afternoons and then at the Jokers Three on Sunday night.

THE Castaways
GREENSBORO, N. C.

For Your Dancing & Entertainment Pleasure

Presents:

STAG: Tuesdays:
Thursdays: **The Fabulous Five**

Sundays: 2 to 6 **The Fabulous Five**

6 to Midnight: **Maurice and the Rebels**

Couples Only:
Friday – Sept. 18th · · · · THE MONZAS
Saturday – Sept. 19th · · · · THE TROPICS

Friday – Sept. 25th · · · · THE PLAYBOYS
Saturday – Sept. 26th · · · · THE CASUALS

Friday – Oct. 2nd · · · · THE EMBERS
Saturday – Oct. 3rd · · · · THE ASCOTS

Friday – Oct. 9th · · · · THE WEEJUNS
Saturday – Oct. 10th · · · · THE DAZZLERS

THE **CASTAWAYS**
GREENSBORO, N. C.
1011 Arnold St. Phone 273-7225

THIS CERTIFICATE, WHEN PRESENTED AT THE CASTAWAYS, GOOD FOR ONE HALF COVER CHARGE. LIMIT OF ONE PER CUSTOMER, NOT VALID ON SUNDAY. OFFER EXPIRES OCTOBER 10, 1964.

LOCATION: Located four blocks behind Eckerds Drug, Northeast Shopping Center, Between Bessemer Avenue and Wendover Avenue.

The Kings Arms Ltd. featured some of the hottest groups in 1963 (they were not yet known as Beach Music groups—it was 1965 before the term Beach Music caught on). The Monzas, Jetty Jumpers, and Bob Collins and the Fabulous Five were featured in October.

KINGS ARMS LTD.

Chapel Hill Blvd. Phone 489-9696

Across from Bowling Alley

Live Entertainment Nightly

Week of Oct. 6th to 10th

Tues	Happy Hour 5 till 12
	Chasers
Wed	Bob Collins
	Fabulous Five
Thur	Monzas
Fri	Monzas
Sat	Jetty Jumpers

Denson Printing Co., Durham, N. C.

Myrtle Beach

PAVILION

★★★ Presents ★★★

ROCK 'N' ROLL

July 24th
THE VILLAGERS

July 26th-27th-28th
THE PLAIDS

July 29th
THE ALPACAS

July 30th-31st
THE GALAXIES

Every Nite
DANCE & SHOW
Begin at 8:15 p.m. to Midnight

also

The Famous Koehlers
"WATER SPORTCADE"
Spectacular Triple High Dive
75 ft. into 7 ft. of water
ADMISSION: Child 25¢
and Adults 80¢ (Incl. tax)

PLUS

The COAST'S
BIGGEST

AMUSEMENT PARK

OPEN DAILY AT 10 A.M.
Every Day
SUNDAY - 1 P.M.

PAVILION
OPEN 24 HOURS A DAY

ON THE OCEAN FRONT
Ocean Blvd. at 9th Ave. N.
MYRTLE BEACH, S. C.

In the summer of 1963, the Myrtle Beach Pavilion featured several rock-and-roll bands. The Villagers, the Plaids, and the Alpacas were all featured and, of course, Harry Deal and the Galaxies, a favorite at the Pavilion since 1959. All of them were later known as Beach Music bands.

The Tiger

"He Roars For Clemson University"

South Carolina's Oldest College Newspaper

Circulation—7,000   CLEMSON, SOUTH CAROLINA, FRIDAY, AUGUST 27, 1965   Vol. LIX—No. 1

Temptations, Barbara Lewis Kick-Off CDA Dance Season

CDA Announces Place, Time, Cost Of Tickets

Performing for the CDA mixer tomorrow are Bob Meyer and the Rivieras. The group operates out of Charlotte, North Carolina.

TOMORROW NIGHT

Rivieras Headline Freshman Mixer

Flu Shots Scheduled For September 14th

There was always great entertainment at Clemson University. The August 27, 1965, *Tiger* featured the Temptations, Barbara Lewis, Bob Meyer and the Rivieras of Charlotte, and the Four Seasons. (Clemson *Tiger*, courtesy of Special Collections in the Strom Thurmond Institute, Clemson University.)

The Wingtips

'6 Piece Combo'

If you would like to have this combo play for your party or school function contact

Charles Clark

Clarkton

Beach Music legends the Wingtips from Clarkton, North Carolina, are seen on October 6, 1965. They played the White Lake region and numerous festivals in the mid-1960s. They also recorded a version of the beach classic "Ain't No Big Thing" on Poverty Records. (Courtesy of the *Southeastern Times*, Elizabethtown, North Carolina.)

Cecil Corbett, then of Tabor City, North Carolina, started offering live bands in the old Shrine Club on U.S. Highway 17 in Myrtle Beach in the summer of 1961. By 1963, he built a larger club just up the road from the original site. By 1971, Cecil formed Beach Club Promotions to book national acts in Florida and the Carolinas. This 1967 schedule resonates with the nostalgia of some of the greatest names in Beach Music. (Itinerary courtesy of "Big Daddy" Wayne Graham.)

SUMMER SPECTACULAR

The Impacts every Monday Night
this Summer

JUNE	3	The Shifters
	7	The Hysterics
	10	The Soul Kings
	14	Showmen and The Monzas
	17	The In-Men
	21	The Cavaliers
	24	The Checkmates
	28	The Hysterics
JULY	1	The Monzas
	5	The In-Men
	8	Soul Inc.
	12	Showmen and The Hysterics
	15	The Checkmates
	19	The Monzas
	22	Maurice Williams, Zodiacs
	26	The In-Men
	29	The Hysterics
AUG.	2	The Manhattens
	5	The Monzas
	9	The Checkmates
	12	The In-Men
	16	The Cavaliers
	19	The Hysterics
	23	The Checkmates
	26	The Manhattens
	31	Showmen and the Hysterics

Although he didn't own it, Cecil Corbett was also closely aligned with the Coachman and Four Club on Highway 401 near Bennettsville, South Carolina. He booked bands for both venues, which made it easier on the bands in travel time, since the clubs were only about 70 miles apart. This was the "Summer Spectacular" lineup for 1967. (Courtesy of A. L. West.)

Charlotte's Catalinas' first appearance at Wilmington College was February 1967. Pictured from left to right are Tommy Black, bassist Sidney Smith, Tommy Plyler, Johnny Edwards (with his back to the camera), and Tom Garner. (Wilmington College *Fledgling*, courtesy of University of North Carolina at Wilmington Archives and Special Collections.)

Wilmington College's homecoming weekend took place in January 1968. The Saturday dance featured the In-Men Ltd. The Friday dance featured the Tropics, the Drifters, and the Robinson Brothers. As the front-line singers for the Tropics, the Robinson Brothers were the "pepper" of one of the few "salt and pepper" groups in that era. Arnold Robinson later joined international super-group the Nylons. (Photograph courtesy of the University of North Carolina at Wilmington Archives and Special Collections.)

Atlantic Records issued the first official Beach Music LP in 1967, including "Drinkin' Wine Spo-Dee-O-Dee" and other beachdigger tunes: "Think A Little Sugar" by Barbara Lewis (with the flip side, "Hello Stranger") and "Thank You John" and "Walking Up a One-Way Street" by Willie Tee.

Doug Clark and The Hot Nuts

A fraternity favorite for years, Doug Clark and the Hot Nuts played the First Blueberry Festival at White Lake, North Carolina, on July 5, 1967. (Courtesy of *Southeastern Times*, Elizabethtown, North Carolina.)

The Boar and Castle, featured in the 1968 Grimsely Senior High annual *Whirligig*, was still the gathering place for Beach Music devotees. The late Lacey Moore of Greensboro, North Carolina, learned to do steps that would become the Shag from carhop Emzie Caldwell in the same Boar and Castle parking lot in 1938.

ELECTRONICALLY RE-RECORDED TO SIMULATE STEREO

THE CLOVERS Nip Sip · LENNY O'HENRY Across The Street · WILLIE TEE Teasin' You
KING CURTIS & THE KINGPINS Memphis Soul Stew · MAURICE WILLIAMS & THE ZODIACS May I
CLYDE McPHATTER Without Love (There Is Nothing) THE COASTERS Idol With The Golden Head
BILLY STEWART Fat Boy · BARBARA LEWIS Hello Stranger · BEN E. KING I (Who Have Nothing)
BOBBY MOORE & THE RHYTHM ACES Searching For My Love · TONY CLARKE The Entertainer

BEACH BEAT VOL. 2 ATLANTIC

After the first album was so well received, the second Beach Music album, again by Atlantic Records, was released in 1968 featuring more beach-exclusive classics: "Across the Street" by Lenny O'Henry, "Teasin' You" by Willie Tee, "Fat Boy" by Billy Stewart, Tony Clarke's "The Entertainer," and Maurice Williams and the Zodiacs' "May I"—a tune that became a huge hit for Bill Deal and the Rhondels of Virginia Beach about 18 months later.

Wilmington College was a hotbed of Beach Music in 1966. In February, the Embers of Raleigh played there, while the Shirelles appeared with Charlotte's Tempests in January. (Wilmington College *Fledgling*, courtesy of University of North Carolina at Wilmington Archives and Special Collections.)

At rehearsal the Tempests prepare for the dance to come. Saturday night the band, a crowd favorite, backed the Shirelles, who sang many of their all-time favorites.

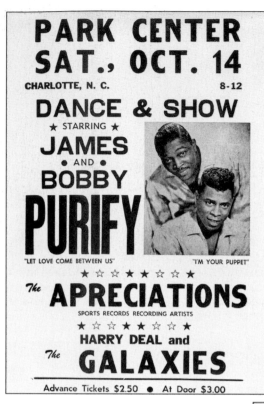

PARK CENTER
SAT., OCT. 14
CHARLOTTE, N. C.   8-12
DANCE & SHOW
★ STARRING ★
JAMES
• AND •
BOBBY
PURIFY
"LET LOVE COME BETWEEN US"   "I'M YOUR PUPPET"
★ ☆ ★ ☆ ★ ☆ ★ ☆ ★
The APRECIATIONS
SPORTS RECORDS RECORDING ARTISTS
★ ☆ ★ ☆ ★ ☆ ★
HARRY DEAL and
The GALAXIES
Advance Tickets $2.50 ● At Door $3.00

The Park Center in Charlotte was the proving ground for many up-and-coming Beach Music groups. Ted Hall and Hit Attractions put together numerous shows there several times a year throughout the 1960s. Every show had a national headliner and local groups; this show on October 14, 1967, included the Appreciations (one of several groups managed by Chatty Hattie of WGIV). Rusty Page of WGIV was the official emcee for the Park Center shows for many years.

On June 7, 1967, the Shirelles were headliners along with Maurice Williams and the Zodiacs, who had reached well beyond local status with "Little Darlin'," a giant hit covered by the Diamonds, and "Stay," Maurice's own huge hit in 1960. The Spontanes, from various parts of North Carolina and Danville, Virginia, were also on the show. They became a split-personality group years later, appearing at their gigs as both the Spontanes and their alter ego, Harley Hogg and the Rockers.

PARK CENTER
WED., JUNE 7
CHARLOTTE, N. C.   8:30-1
DANCE & SHOW
★ ☆ STARRING THE ☆ ★
SHIRELLES
★ ☆ ★
MAURICE
WILLIAMS ZODIACS
AND THE
★ ☆ ★
The SPONTANES

A rare photograph of the corner stage at the Castaways Club in Greensboro shows Kallabash Corporation in 1969; from left to right are Tommy Coleman, Ken Helser, Ronnie Purcell on bass behind him, Bo Williams, Leo Caudle, Mark Wrenn, and Ted Keaton on keyboards. (Photograph courtesy of Ted Keaton.)

Another of the great Beach Music bands of the 1960s, the In-Men Ltd., is seen at Wilmington College in 1968. (Wilmington College 1968 *Fledgling*, courtesy of University of North Carolina at Wilmington Archives and Special Collections.)

APRIL SCHEDULE
AT
THE CELLAR
300 E. Morehead St. Charlotte — Phone 375-9151

WED.	Apr.	2 —	The SCRIBES (Ladies Night)
FRI.	Apr.	4 —	The COLLEGIATES
SAT.	Apr.	5 —	The TYMES
SUN.	Apr.	6 —	The SLAVES
WED.	Apr.	9 —	The HYSTERICS (Ladies Night)
FRI.	Apr.	11 —	The DIABLOS
SAT.	Apr.	12 —	The CASTAWAYS
SUN.	Apr.	13 —	The SOUL SEEKERS
WED.	Apr.	16 —	The MARLBOROS (Ladies Night)
THUR.	Apr.	17 —	AUGUST
FRI.	Apr.	18 —	FRATERNITY, INC.
SAT.	Apr.	19 —	The CASUALS
SUN.	Apr.	20 —	The CATALINAS 4:00 - 7:00
SUN. Nite	Apr.	20 —	The GEORGIA PROPHETS 8:00 - 11:30
WED.	Apr.	23 —	The NOVAS 9 (Ladies Night)
FRI.	Apr.	25 —	The FLARES
SAT.	Apr.	26 —	Gene Barbour & the Cavaliers
SUN.	Apr.	27 —	The KALLABASH
WED.	Apr.	30 —	The COLLEGIATES

OPEN WEEK-DAYS 4:30 - 11:45   OPEN SUNDAYS 2:30 - 11:45

THE CELLAR
"Often Imitated - Never Duplicated"
— PLEASE BRING I. D. —   ALL DATES SUBJECT TO CHANGE

MAY SCHEDULE
AT
THE CELLAR
300 E. Morehead St. Charlotte — Phone 375-9151

FRI.	May	2 —	The CASUALS
SAT.	May	3 —	The TYMES
SUN.	May	4 —	GEORGIA PROPHETS
WED.	May	7 —	The MARLBOROS (Ladies Night)
FRI.	May	9 —	The SANDS
SAT.	May	10 —	The PERFECTIONS Backed By The SCRIBES
SUN.	May	11 —	Billy Stewart Revue
WED.	May	14 —	The COLLEGIATES (Ladies Night)
FRI.	May	16 —	The DIABLOS
SAT.	May	17 —	The Fabulous Affairs
SUN. AFTERNOON (4-7)	May	18 —	Willie Tee & Magnificents
SUN. NITE	May	18 —	The CATALINAS 8:00 - 11:30
WED.	May	21 —	The KALLABASH (Ladies Night)
FRI.	May	23 —	The HYSTERICS
SAT.	May	24 —	The PERFECTIONS Backed By C.C. & The SOULS
SUN.	May	25 —	GEORGIA PROPHETS
WED.	May	28 —	The COLLEGIATES (Ladies Night)
FRI.	May	30 —	The FLARES
SAT.	May	31 —	The TYMES

OPEN WEEK-DAYS 4:30 - 11:45   OPEN SUNDAYS 2:30 - 11:45

THE CELLAR
"Often Imitated - Never Duplicated"
— PLEASE BRING I. D. —   ALL DATES SUBJECT TO CHANGE

SEPTEMBER SCHEDULE
AT
THE CELLAR
300 E. Morehead St. Charlotte — Phone 375-9151

WED.	Sept.	3 —	The CAPRIS (Ladies Night)
FRI.	Sept.	5 —	Men Of Distinction
SAT.	Sept.	6 —	C. C. and The SOULS
SUN.	Sept.	7 —	BILLY, BARBARA & BILLY (Georgia's Best)
WED.	Sept.	10 —	The MARLBOROS (Ladies Night)
FRI.	Sept.	12 —	O'BANYAN & The FEATURES
SAT.	Sept.	13 —	The COLLEGIATES
SUN.	Sept.	14 —	BILLY, BARBARA & BILLY (Georgia's Best)
WED.	Sept.	17 —	The IMPACTS (Ladies Night)
FRI.	Sept.	19 —	The FLARES
SAT.	Sept.	20 —	The POOR SOULS
SUN.	Sept.	21 —	THE SPIRAL STAIRCASE & The Men Of DISTINCTION
WED.	Sept.	24 —	The COLLEGIATES (LADIES NIGHT)
FRI.	Sept.	26 —	The FABULOUS AFFAIRS
SAT.	Sept.	27 —	The LOOKING GLASS
SUN.	Sept.	28 —	IN - MEN & The CATALINAS SHOW BEGINS at 6:00 P.M.

OPEN WEEK-DAYS 4:30 - 11:45   OPEN SUNDAYS 2:30 - 11:45

THE CELLAR
"Often Imitated - Never Duplicated"
— PLEASE BRING I. D. —   ALL DATES SUBJECT TO CHANGE

Larry Presley's well-known Cellar opened in 1965 and offered nickel drafts on Sundays for years. The Cellar was said to have the coldest beer in the Carolinas. Billy Scott and the Georgia Prophets recorded part of their live album in the Cellar, as did Soul Inc. out of Columbia. The Cellar era ended in 1971, when it became Country Underground. Chris Beachley of the Wax Museum in Charlotte said the Cellar jukebox was such an important part of his education that he'd go there on off nights so he could hear "Hey There Lonely Boy" by Ruby and the Romantics echoing off the walls. He said the Cellar gave him his first tastes of Earl Bostic, Bob Collins and the Fabulous Five, "Drunk" by Jimmy Liggins, "Not Too Long Ago" by the Uniques, and "Pennies from Heaven" by the Skyliners. (Courtesy of the Wax Museum, Charlotte.)

Many of the biggest and best beach bands were playing at the Shelby Teen Club in Shelby City Park in 1968. The Embers still perform in 2005, as do the Attractions, who reformed in the new millennium. (Playbills courtesy of Mary Blanton.)

The Raleigh auditorium was one of the great venues for what became Beach Music. Charlotte's Tempests, with a hot new LP in the summer of 1968, played the Pavilion in August. In March 1968, the Park Center featured Jay and the Techniques and the Flares Revue, a group that included Alicia Bridges ("I Love the Nightlife," 1978). Billy Stewart played the Stallion in August. (Pavilion poster courtesy of Roger Branch; Stallion Club poster courtesy of Julian Fowler.)

Although Robert Honeycutt's last night was New Year's Eve 1969, there were still great headliners playing Williams Lake that fall. The Tempests and Embers played the Ocean Plaza at Carolina Beach in April 1969. Boot's Upstairs Club in Spartanburg was another hot spot around 1970. On the coast in 1971 was the Barrel (sometimes known as Jap's Barrel or Buck's Barrel) at North Myrtle Beach. (The Barrel poster courtesy of Dan Duvall.)

There's no way to describe all the graffiti on the walls of the Beach Party. This beloved joint was across the horseshoe from the Ocean Drive (O. D.) Pavilion. The Beach Party was the proving ground for Richard Nixon, one of the first DJs in the hall of fame at Fat Harold's, just up the street. The Beach Party's name was changed many times. Today the O. D. Beach and Golf Resort, the Spanish Galleon, and the O. D. Beach Club sit in the same spot. (Photograph courtesy of Mickey Maness.)

Billy Stewart—the Fat Boy—plays at the legendary Cellar in Charlotte in 1969. Billy started out in the Rainbows with Don Covay and Marvin Gaye in Washington, D.C. On the national scene, Billy is best known for his hit "Summertime." On the Beach Music scene, he's revered for songs like "Fat Boy," "I Do Love You," "Sitting In the Park," "Look Back and Smile," and "A Fat Boy Can Cry." Impresario Larry Presley launched the reign of the Cellar from 1965 to 1971. (Photograph courtesy of Van Elrod.)

The Lake Lure Inn in North Carolina has enjoyed three incarnations as a venue for Shag and Beach Music. It is reputed to have been the site of the first live Carolinas big band radio broadcast in the 1940s. In the 1960s, the El Tango club offered entertainment by Ted Hall's Hit Attractions out of Charlotte, as demonstrated by this April 17, 1965 poster (below). The Lake Lure area was used in much of the filming of *Dirty Dancing* in 1987, starring Jennifer Grey and Patrick Swayze. Although the story is loosely based on the real-life experiences of Eleanor Bergstein in the Catskills holiday camps during her youth, the dirty dancing done to Solomon Burke's "Cry To Me" and "Do You Love Me" by the Contours was reminiscent of the dirty Shag done in the Carolinas since the 1940s. (Playbill courtesy of Rocky Phillips.)

EL TANGO
SAT., APRIL 17
LAKE LURE, N. C. 8—12
DANCE & SHOW
★ STARRING ★
THE DELMONICOS
& THEIR
ORCHESTRA
a **HIT** attraction
CHARLOTTE THEATRICAL PRINTING CO.

The Jolly Knave originated in Atlantic Beach, North Carolina, in 1971. Vinton Fountain of Tarboro, North Carolina, and Fred Fletcher of Raleigh were the original owners. Their first Shag contest was held in 1974. Linda Cook and Danny Bean were the winners. Bill Harper, an Eastern Carolina University graduate from Rocky Mount, bought the club in 1978. The Shag contests continued through 1984. In 1986, changes were made with a smaller lounge but still with a dance floor and Beach Music. (Photograph courtesy of Bill Harper.)

As a kid, Larry Sprinkle listened to WAAA in Winston-Salem in the 1950s and 1960s. While at Eastern Carolina University in Greenville, North Carolina, he worked at WOOW radio, where in 1968 he was the first to play a tape of "Girl Watcher" before it was a record and before the recording group was called the O'Kaysions. He was Sandy Beach on the *Sandy Beach Show* on Big WAYS from 1972 to 1985. Today Sandy Beach has resumed his real name as a weatherman in Charlotte. (Photograph courtesy of Larry Sprinkle.)

University of South Carolina students knew there was one place to see and be seen, to Shag and be Shagged: the Tally-Ho Club. People still talk about the great jukebox with "I've Been Waiting" by Cortez Grier and the Lifters, Don Cherry's "Lucky Old Sun," "Lonely Drifter" by the Pieces of Eight, "Ol' Man River" by the Ravens, "If We Had to Do It All Over" by Sunny and Phyllis, and many others. (Photograph courtesy of Lenny A. Lipscomb; jukebox history courtesy of Guerry Sample and Jerry Timms.)

This building was heaven to locals in the Statesville, Hickory, and Troutman areas of North Carolina in the 1960s. It was known as George's. The Isley Brothers' huge 1973 hit, "That Lady" on T-Neck Records, was originally a smooth Shag tune on United Artists Records entitled "Who's That Lady" that could be found on the George's jukebox in 1965. (Photograph courtesy of Bill Raymer; jukebox history courtesy of Randy Rowland.)

Beach Music of the 1960s and 1970s was sweet soul, while Beach Music of the 1940s and 1950s was swing and early rhythm and blues. The 1960s was the golden age of Beach Music. Motown was queen and the Philadelphia sound was a big player. At Fat Jack's 1979 Fall Shag contest in North Myrtle Beach, Mike Lewis was the DJ who unveiled a heady mix of jump blues that has pushed the envelope of Shag music ever since. (Photograph courtesy of S.O.S.)

Chris Beachley ("Dr. Beachley") opened the Wax Museum in Charlotte in 1972. Chris had cut his teeth on beach tunes on the Cellar jukebox and wanted to own them all—he ended up with nearly a million. In 1976, he was practically twisting arms to get people to listen to "Ms Grace" by the Tymes, which became one of the five biggest beach hits of all time. Dr. Beachley is pictured in front of the 24-year location at 1505 Elizabeth Avenue.

Several judges at Groucho's Beach Club's 1981 Fall Shag contest were later inducted into the Shaggers Hall of Fame. From left to right in the front, they are Glenda Johnson, Chuck Mack, Peggy Mack in the back, Ham McGarity, H. Lee Brown (standing), Judy McDougal in checkered sweater, Sandra Schwartz, Darby McDougal (the little girl), Donna Schaffer (seated), Elliott Schwartz partially hidden behind Schaffer, Charles Gurley, Charles Jernigan (facing front), and Buzz Sawyer (seated far right). In the DJ booth are Chris Beachley and Ervin Barum. (Photograph courtesy of Randy Rowland.)

Groucho's opened October 1977. When Randy Rowland purchased half ownership along with Tom Wicker in January 1978, it became a beach club and then moved to its second location in September 1980. (Photograph courtesy of Randy Rowland.)

In 1980, hall-of-famer Billy Waldrep and friends suggested to the Tramps' management in Greenville, South Carolina, that they'd do well with a Shag contest that ran every Wednesday night for four to six weeks. Dancers came from everywhere in the Carolinas, and the big cash contests began, to culminate with a $25,000 contest at the Mirage Beach Club in Charleston in the early 1980s.

Fat Harold's first annual Shag contest was at his H.A.T.S. club (Harold's Across the Street) in the old Barrel on Ocean Boulevard. By 1982, there were so many competing contests that club owners joined together as the Shaggers Preservation Association (S.P.A.). There were seven S.P.A. clubs, including Sh-Booms in Fayetteville; Fat Jack's in North Myrtle Beach; Fat Harold's Across the Street in North Myrtle Beach; Groucho's in Charlotte; Ocean Drive North in Rocky Mount; Sand Flea in Greenville, South Carolina; and Bushes in Greensboro.

Johnny Dollar's celebrated a reunion of Papa Doc's, another great—but short-lived—beach club of Charlotte, which was also on South Boulevard in the early 1970s. They celebrated with the Hot Nuts band, a Shag contest, and a chug contest.

The original Johnny Dollar's was opened by Tom Wicker on South Boulevard in Charlotte around 1975. "Ms Grace" was the hottest song on the jukebox throughout the summer of 1975. In 1980, Bob Whitman took over and moved it to a new location on Old Pineville Road. While Johnny Dollar's was under Bob's guidance, Bill Bradford and Sandy Bell wrote a song entitled "(They Call It) Mr. Dollars" that would eventually become a Beach Music standard.

Cagney's is a Myrtle Beach restaurant and nightclub that enjoyed its heyday as a Shag gathering place in the 1980s. It's still a great restaurant, co-owned by Dino Drosas and his partner, Dino Thompson. Just before the legendary Ocean Forest Hotel was imploded on September 13, 1974, Thompson arranged for a lot of the decorative wall and ceiling materials to be transferred to and made part of Cagney's. In the early 1980s, Cagney's celebrated the tradition to which it belonged with this great poster.

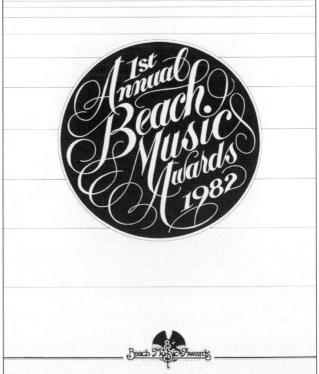

The First Beach Music Awards in 1982 had such a profound impact on Beach Music that they've never really stopped, although they've continued under different names and owners but still with the same general trajectory. John X. Aragona of Virginia Beach was the executive producer of the first, second, and third awards shows.

Four

S.O.S.

Celebration of the
Carefree Lifestyle

Two important rites of passage on the edge were watching the dirty Shag and doing the dirty Shag, both depicted in this original drawing by Becky Stowe. (Drawing courtesy of Becky Stowe at Beach Memories, North Myrtle Beach; and S.O.S.)

North Myrtle Beach mayor Joseph J. Saleeby declared September 11 through 16, 1980, S.O.S. Week, and it has been going and growing ever since. (Photograph courtesy of S.O.S. and the Association of Carolina Shag Clubs. Learn more about S.O.S. activities and history at www.Shagdance.com.)

The impetus for the Society of Shaggers (S.O.S.) was an elaborate joke by Gene "Swink" Laughter, in which a message in a bottle washed ashore with a call for assistance for the USS *Raven*. While a few historians and newspapers scrambled to determine the note's authenticity, Gene and friends were organizing a get-together for the beach boys and girls of the 1940s and 1950s. (Photograph courtesy of S.O.S. and the Association of Carolina Shag Clubs.)

104

South Carolina governor Dick Riley signed the proclamation making the Shag the state dance on April 6, 1984. Rep. John "Bubber" Snow (D–Williamsburg), the driving force behind the bill, was a Shaggers Hall of Fame member and dance enthusiast of the first order. Representative Snow was also responsible for the declaration of Beach Music as the state's popular music on March 27, 2001. Myrtle Beach artist Cheryl Allred designed the Shag logo for South Carolina in 1986.

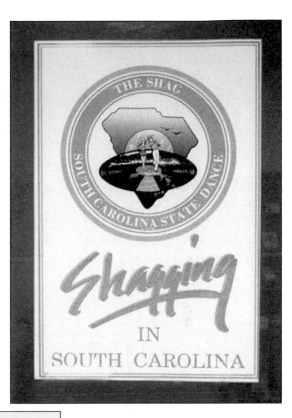

S.O.S. Extends the Celebration
1994 Spring Safari to begin on April 15th.
Fall Migration on September 9th.
Ten full days each.

S.O.S. goes to ten-day format
for Spring and Fall—more days, more fun!

Heads Up, Shaggers, Stranders, Lovers of the Beach–S.O.S. is going to give you five more days to enjoy the beach, strand, music, and shagging. Five more days to ease your accommodations problem, traffic tie ups, parking dilemmas, and dance floor space.

Stranders have begun coming to S.O.S. on the week-end before the official dates for years. It's time we accommodate them. Beginning in 1994, the entire ten-day period will be an S.O.S. event only. Participating clubs will require the S.O.S. card for admission from April 15th thru April 24th. This will assure all of us that this is a week-end completely committed to the strand, shag, and S.O.S.

To ease your access to the participating clubs during the entire ten-day periods, S.O.S. memberships will be available from each club whenever they are open beginning with the New Year's Day week-end. Beginning with the Spring Safari, S.O.S. membership cards will be sold at the beach by participating clubs only. S.O.S. will open an information headquarters during the event, but membership cards will not be sold there. Membership cards will continue to be available through the mail as usual.

Your S.O.S. Officers and Board of Directors listen to your comments and suggestions regarding the finest adult party in the entire country. Please continue to let us know what you think. We are always interested.

S.O.S. Spring Safari and Fall Migration were extended to 10 days each in 1994. This doesn't count the big mid-winter party in January, which, although not an S.O.S. event, is related because it is sponsored by the Association of Carolina Shag Clubs. There is also a Junior S.O.S. event every July and innumerable two- and three-day weekends sponsored by the 100-plus Shag and bop clubs in the Association. (Photograph courtesy of S.O.S. and the Association of Carolina Shag Clubs.)

WRDX 106.5 FM started as X-106 in Salisbury, North Carolina, in 1986—the first full-time Beach Music station in history. North Myrtle Beach artist Becky Stowe of Beach Memories captured the core crew in this painting. From left to right are Dave Landon, Rod Harter, April McIntyre (daughter of Hal McIntyre, mentioned earlier), Phil Kehr, and John Hook. Beach 106 lasted until the spring of 1995.

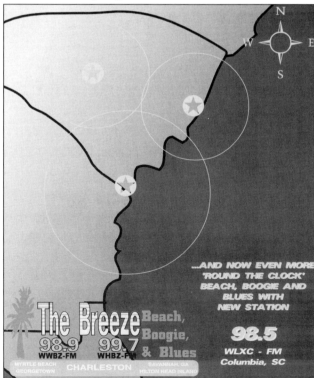

Just as Beach 106 was waning, the Breeze Network, brainchild of Frank Baker and the Windham brothers, Woody and Leo, was waxing. The Breeze was a simulcast concept that ended in 2001 with four stations covering South Carolina, part of Georgia, and Wilmington, North Carolina. The Breeze included the late and beloved Eddie Zomerfeld, "EZ" to his many listeners, who also performed with Soul Incorporated, a Columbia beach band in the 1960s. (Map courtesy of S.O.S.)

Following the demise of the Breeze Network, the Boogie Beach Radio Network was launched from Columbia with, from left to right. Eddie Zomerfeld, John Smith, Jim Bowers, and Dave Carr. (Photograph courtesy of Barry Thigpen/National Shag Dance Championships.)

The Association of Beach and Shag Club DJs (ABSCDJs) had its beginnings among several important DJs in 1984 in Chapel Hill and was formally chartered in the 1990s at Atlantic Beach, North Carolina. They supply the majority of the DJs for S.O.S. functions, Association of Carolina Shag Club (ACSC) functions, and other parties.

THE ASSOCIATION OF DJ
BEACH & SHAG CLUB D.J.'s

Unless one showed up for one of Bill Griffin's Sunday-night cook-outs at the Bushes (giant shrimp, spaghetti, burgers, steaks, pork chops, and more) and stayed to dance on the postage-stamp-sized floor, then one never really lived the carefree life. It was a small dance floor, but the legendary smooth steppers who danced there never needed a warehouse anyway. (Photograph courtesy of John Cottingham; his lovely wife, Kaye, is leading the blindfolded Shagger in the foreground.)

Few of the infamous murals or walls of graffiti, like this one at Ducks Across the Street in 1987, still exist. The Pad, Bushes, Thirsty's, and Beach Music Cafe, all in Myrtle Beach, have all disappeared. (Photograph courtesy of Wanda Martin.)

Barry Thigpen put together the National Shag Dance Championships in 1984 in response to a request from the Myrtle Beach Chamber of Commerce to create something exciting. Studebakers in Myrtle Beach was the nationals' headquarters for most of the first 20 years. Television hostess Diane DeVaughn Stokes has been emcee throughout with professional DJ assistance from Judy Collins of Judy's House of Oldies in North Myrtle Beach. (Annuals and brochures provided courtesy of the National Shag Championships, thanks to Barry Thigpen.)

Charlie Womble and Jackie McGee, nine-time champions together (Jackie later added a 10th win to her resume), are pictured on the 10th anniversary National Shag Dance Championships program cover in 1993. Charlie and Jackie have also been ambassadors of Shag across America for decades. (Annuals provided courtesy of the National Shag Championships, thanks to Barry Thigpen.)

While shooting *Days of Thunder* in the Carolinas with Tom Cruise, Robert Duvall was captivated by the Shag. A tango enthusiast of the first order, Duvall studied with Shad and Brenda Alberty for several months during filming. As shown here at far right, Duvall attended and danced at the 1990 National Shag Championships at Studebakers in Myrtle Beach. (Photograph courtesy of Ervin "Dr. Shag" Ellington.)

The 19th edition of the nationals was also a celebration of 10 years of the National Shag Dance Teams. (Annuals provided courtesy of the National Shag Championships, thanks to Barry Thigpen.)

Five

THE SHAG AND BEACH MUSIC CHRONICLES

Beach Music was 60 years old in 2005. No one noticed it was evolving in 1945 or 1955 or 1965. Fortunately, in 1979, Dr. Beachley (Chris Beachley) began documenting the songs in charts and reports from the major Shag contests. This chart is from 1993.

The first Beach Music magazine debuted in 1979 as a result of Dr. Beachley's receipt of requests for more information regarding Shag contests. *It Will Stand* featured General Johnson and his Showmen and Chairmen, Willie Tee from New Orleans, Amos Milburn, and Archie Bell and the Drells. Issues five through seven were comprised of a three-part Drifters history. Each issue was packed with Shag contest news, record reviews, and special reminiscing columns. Other featured artists included Dinah Washington, the Blenders, the Tempests, Frank Culley, and Billy Scott and the Georgia Prophets.

It Will Stand was named in honor of the Showmen's first beach hit in 1962. Issues featured Edwin Starr, the Platters, Billy Stewart, Billy Butler, and Janice Barnett. Earl Bostic was spotlighted, as well as Sunny and Phyllis from Spartanburg, Ruth Brown and the Artistics, the Catalinas, the Penguins, Jackie Ross, the Grand Strand Band, Spirit Records' Bradford and Bell, and the first Beach Music Awards. *It Will Stand* ended with Issue Number 36. (*It Will Stand* issues courtesy of Dr. Beachley.)

Other magazines came and went during the *It Will Stand* era. One volume of *Sounds of the Sands* was issued in July 1980. *It's Shag Time* was a three-issue publication in January, February, and March 1982. Written by several dancers, it was dedicated to "The Best of the Old and New Dance."

Headliners newspaper, published by Ron Ramsey of Lincolnton, North Carolina, enjoyed at least 30 volumes. Ron did a great job of covering the beach bands. He also covered other genres of entertainment. Included in the paper were Charlotte's Spongetones, a very Beatles-oriented rock group. *The Music Paper*, a Charlotte magazine published by "Brother Dave" Freeman, may have been a model for *Headliners*. Dave's publication covered all aspects of music and performance in the Metrolina area for 15 years—before and after *Headliners*.

113

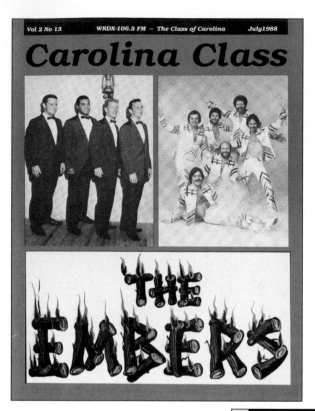

Beach 106 launched *Carolina Class* in the spring of 1987. The first issue covered Bill Griffin's Beach, Boogie, and Blues Fest in Jamestown, North Carolina. The July 1988 issue featured the history of the Embers of Raleigh with pictures and information about some of their very earliest records that hadn't been reported previously.

Carolina Class also aimed to fill the void covering the bands left by *Headliners* after its demise in 1985. Shown here is Maurice Williams in the November 1988 issue. Altogether there were 36 published issues of *Carolina Class* and one very collectible issue that was never officially published.

The Mighty WLWL of Rockingham, North Carolina, captained by Kebo Davis, started its *77WL Beach Connection* in 1989 and offered Beach Music and Shag news for at least two years.

Dancing on the Edge introduced Shag line genealogy, the history of Shag traditions passed along a specific genealogical path. Although a common subject of discussion, it had never been reported in the past.

Rhythm 'n Beach News was published through the summer and fall of 1990. This issue reported the Washington, D.C., concerts and album put on by South Carolinian Lee Atwater, one of the right-hand men of Pres. George Bush Sr. There were stories on Larry and the Loafers of PC (Panama City) Bop fame in the Panama Beach, Florida, area. There was also a story on the sad demise of Sammy Davis Jr.

Beach Music Monthly out of Nashville was published from May through September 1993. It was a slick, color–front cover magazine which started with General Johnson and the Chairmen in May and Charlie and Jackie in June; Becky Stowe provided the God Bless America cover in July, and Bill Pinkney, the last original Drifter, was August's cover. The final issue saluted Beach Music's DJs, especially the new ABSCDJs, whose officers appeared on the cover.

In 1995, after the fall of Beach 106 radio, Curtiss Carpenter and Billy Scott of the Georgia Prophets created the Cammys (nowadays the Carolina Music Awards), which celebrated its 10th year in 2004. The Carolina Music Awards is a fantastic yearly show that has found a home at the Alabama Theatre in North Myrtle Beach each November.

Summer 1994 saw the first issue of *Shagger* magazine. Even slicker than *Beach Music Monthly*, it had color inside as well as on the front cover. Issue Number 4, which was Volume 2 Number 2, featured the supernova of Shaggers, the late Harry Driver from Dunn, North Carolina.

The movie *Shag* was released in 1989. The final dance contest, beloved by many critics and fans alike, was filmed in the Atlantic Beach Pavilion, one of the last of the old-style pavilions on the black beach of the Grand Strand in South Carolina. Not long after the movie was completed, the pavilion burned. Barry Thigpen of the National Shag Dance Championships was instrumental in assisting the stars who danced in the filming of the movie.

The *Shag News Network* was a fun, sometimes irreverent, weekly 30-minute show designed by Will and Tommy Espin of Charlotte, with Al Ross as a roving reporter and 'Fessa John Hook as host. *SNN* was produced in 1990 and 1991. Several television stations were still rerunning the shows two years after *SNN* shut down.

Charlie Womble and Jackie McGee, along with S.O.S., created the first Grand National Dance Championship in Atlanta in May 1995. In the program's introduction, Charlie and Jackie stated, "This weekend you can watch the best swing dancers in the country compete in their respective categories—including Carolina Shag. You can also social dance your style of swing as well as experiment with and learn about other dance styles. The intent of the SOSGNDC [S.O.S. Grand National Dance Championship] is not to change any dance style, but rather to offer each of us an opportunity to improve our dancing through association with dancers who do things a little differently."

May 26 - 28, 1995   Atlanta, GA

They went on to say, "The SOSGNDC is a result of our desire to give each of you the opportunity to experience what has meant so much to Jackie and me over the last six years. That is, the exposure to other forms of dance and to new people with a common interest—the love of music and dancing. Dancing brings many rewards, the greatest of which is friendships. We hope that everyone will make a real effort to make new friends this weekend. You will be richer for the effort."

The Seaboard Shag Contest, in conjunction with the yearly Seaboard Festival in Hamlet, North Carolina, celebrating the heritage of the Atlantic Seaboard Railroad, is a Competitive Shaggers' Association–sponsored event at the Ballroom in Hamlet. Throughout the 1980s, dancers who regularly competed in Shag contests were loosely organized. The Competitive Shaggers' Association (CSA) was organized the fall of 1992 and worked with the Shaggers Preservation Association (SPA) to promote the dance and organize the contests. (History courtesy of Bill Drew and the CSA.)

The founding CSA board is pictured here. Seated front center are Charlie and Linda Reese. Clockwise from left are Kathy Benfield, Pee Wee Teel, Pam Jones, Phil Jones, John Teel, Gene Benfield, Bill Drew, Sharli Drew, and Gale Robertson. Seated on the floor at center is Claude Robertson. (Drawing by Hall of Fame Shagger Bill Young 1992, courtesy of the CSA.)

Fat Harold's Beach Club is on Main Street in North Myrtle Beach, South Carolina. Not only is it the most cherished year-round Shag club there—it is actually two clubs, with two different rooms, each with a gigantic dance floor—Fat Harold also features beach bands from time to time. The whole building could just as easily be called Fat Harold's Beach Museum. Set aside an hour or two to enjoy wall after wall of memorabilia and history. (Photograph courtesy of Mike Rink.)

The Beach Music DJs Hall of Fame takes up two walls in Fat Harold's Beach Club. Many of the great DJs of the past and today are enshrined there.

One of the most fascinating walls in Fat Harold's, right next to the DJ booth in the main dance hall, is dedicated to the lifeguards of the 1950s and 1960s who formed the KMA Club (reportedly Knights of Many Adventures, but the huge lip print with the letters KMA in the picture may be a "hint" as to the true meaning). Many of the KMA's "adventures" are described in words and pictures on this one of many special walls at Fat Harold's. (Photograph courtesy of Fat Harold and David Vaughan.)

Fat Harold's is also home to the O. D. Shag Club. Why O. D.? Long before the area was called North Myrtle Beach, it was described by locals and visitors alike as Ocean Drive. Many refuse to call it North Myrtle Beach to this day. Even Roberts Pavilion was called the O. D. Pavilion, or the Ocean Drive Pavilion, by many.

This is the O. D. Pavilion that replaced Roberts Pavilion in 1955, after Hurricane Hazel. Today it is run by H. Lee and Pam Brown, and it is also known as Pam's Palace. The pavilion is one of the favorite haunts of the O. D. Pavilion Social and Shag Club (ODPSSC). The walls of the pavilion are covered with casual shots of its patrons over the last 10 years and lots of interesting memorabilia as well. (Photograph courtesy of Sara Richardson.)

North Myrtle Beach started the new millennium with a water tower sign announcing the "Soul of NMB—Home of the Shag!"

At the end of Main Street in North Myrtle Beach, on the left side of the horseshoe at the edge of the dunes, is the O. D. Beach and Golf Resort, a hotel that also houses the Spanish Galleon and a Beach Club with an outside deck. The hotel also houses the Museum of the Shaggers Hall of Fame. The biographies of the hall of famers constitute 70 years of dance and music history in the Carolinas. The first inductees in 1983 (above) were, from left to right, top to bottom, Clarice Reavis, Harry Driver, Jean Allen Ferguson, and Billy Jeffers. The other 1983 inductees (below) were, from left to right, top to bottom, Marilyn Hodges, Leon Williams, Weezie Rogers Vickery, and Nelson Burton. (Photograph courtesy of Harold Worley and the Shaggers Hall of Fame.)

Ducks Shag Club has undergone three or four transformations on Main Street since the mid-1980s, when it was started by H. Lee Brown. Today Ducks is the home of a vast variety of Shag and Beach Music memorabilia and a wall dedicated to the "Keepers of the Dance," the young people of today who carry on the Shag tradition. (Photograph courtesy of Cooter Douglas.)

Most of the Keepers of the Dance have at one time or another been involved with the Junior Shaggers and the Junior Shag Association, which has its own Junior S.O.S. event every July. (Photograph courtesy of Mike and Connie Mack, the Boulevard Grill.)

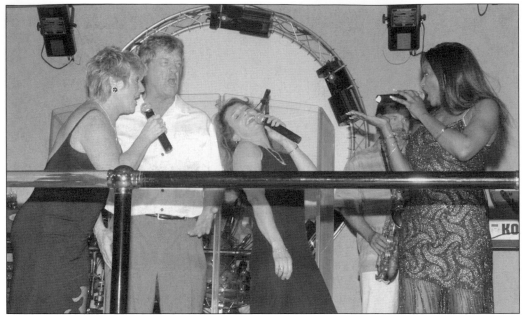

John Hook became an owner of 94.9 FM in Myrtle Beach in 2003. Hook also hosted the afternoon show and *Born In the Carolinas Live* (*BICL*) every Sunday night. On stage for *BICL* are, from left to right, Susan Trexler, John Hook, Terri Gore, Craig Woolard and Linda Johnson.

Along with new partners, Hook expanded his Shag commitments in 2004. Pictured from left to right are Dave Freeman, Wanda Freeman, Kathy Hardwick, and John Hook, who own the Endless Summer Network on the Internet (www.beachShag.com) and 105.3 FM at Myrtle Beach.

This freestyle Shag line includes, from left to right, Buzz Sawyer, Mike Osborne, A. V. Franklin, Alan Tuck (front), Kim Maynard, and John Hook. A. V. Franklin taught Mike Osborne in 1957, who taught Buzz Sawyer and Alan Tuck in the early 1960s; Buzz taught Kim Maynard in the mid-1960s, and Kim taught John Hook in the 1980s.

From left to right, A. V. Franklin, Dreama Osborne, and Mason Parks were well-known dancers at Tony's Lake in China Grove, North Carolina, in the 1950s. A. V. remembered, "Mason was the best dresser, dancer, pool and ping pong player in Kannapolis. I wanted to be just like him, then dethrone him." Mason taught A. V. to dance at the Kannapolis YMCA in 1954.

As long as there are dance floors and music, there's the possibility to rekindle lost loves and resume lost friendships. If we're really lucky, "no broken heart aches with every wave that breaks over love letters in the sand." Instead we'll keep dancing like Marion and Ardis Courtney, who learned to Shag in 1948 and Shagged to the last. Daughter Suzanne said that even when Marion was nearly too weak to walk, he still got up to dance with Ardis. They are Shagging above in April 1992 in New Orleans. Ardis Courtney turned 80 in November 2004. (Photograph courtesy of Suzanne Kennedy; lyrics from "Love Letters In the Sand" by Charles and Nick Kenny and J. Fred Coots.)